# 500 INSECTS

## A VISUAL REFERENCE

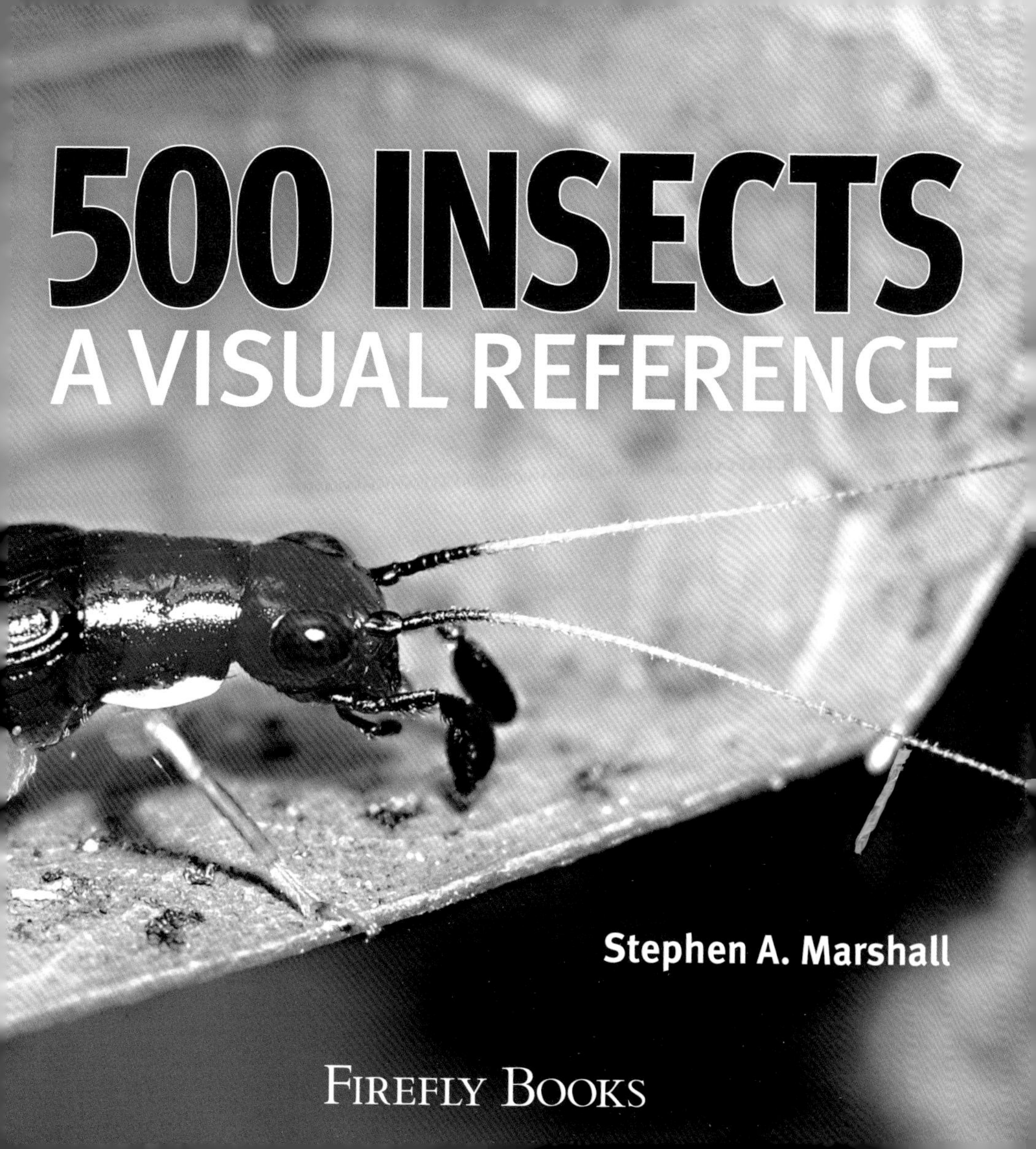

# 500 INSECTS
## A VISUAL REFERENCE

Stephen A. Marshall

FIREFLY BOOKS

A FIREFLY BOOK

Published by Firefly Books Ltd. 2024


First printing

**Library of Congress Control Number**: 2023947519

**Library and Archives Canada Cataloguing in Publication**
Title: 500 insects : a visual reference / Stephen A. Marshall.
Other titles: Five hundred insects
Names: Marshall, S. A. (Stephen A.), author.
Description: Previously published in 2008. |
Includes bibliographical references and index.
Identifiers: Canadiana 20230548873 |
ISBN 9780228104940 (softcover)
Subjects: LCSH: Insects—Identification. |
LCSH: Insects—Pictorial works. | LCGFT: Informational works. |
LCGFT: Illustrated works.
Classification: LCC QL467 .M37 2024 | DDC 595.7—dc23

Published in the United States by
Firefly Books (U.S.) Inc.
P.O. Box 1338, Ellicott Station
Buffalo, New York 14205

Published in Canada by
Firefly Books Ltd.
50 Staples Avenue, Unit 1
Richmond Hill, Ontario L4B 0A7

Cover and interior design by LINDdesign

Printed in China | E

Canadä
*We acknowledge the financial support of the Government of Canada.*

Cover: A Bolivian treehopper (*Cyphonia trifida*)

Half-title page: A tropical treehopper (*Bocydium*)

Title page: Handsome Trig Bush Cricket (*Phyllopalpus pulchellus*)

Opposite: Gall midges (Cecidomyiidae) landing on a leaf in Costa Rica.

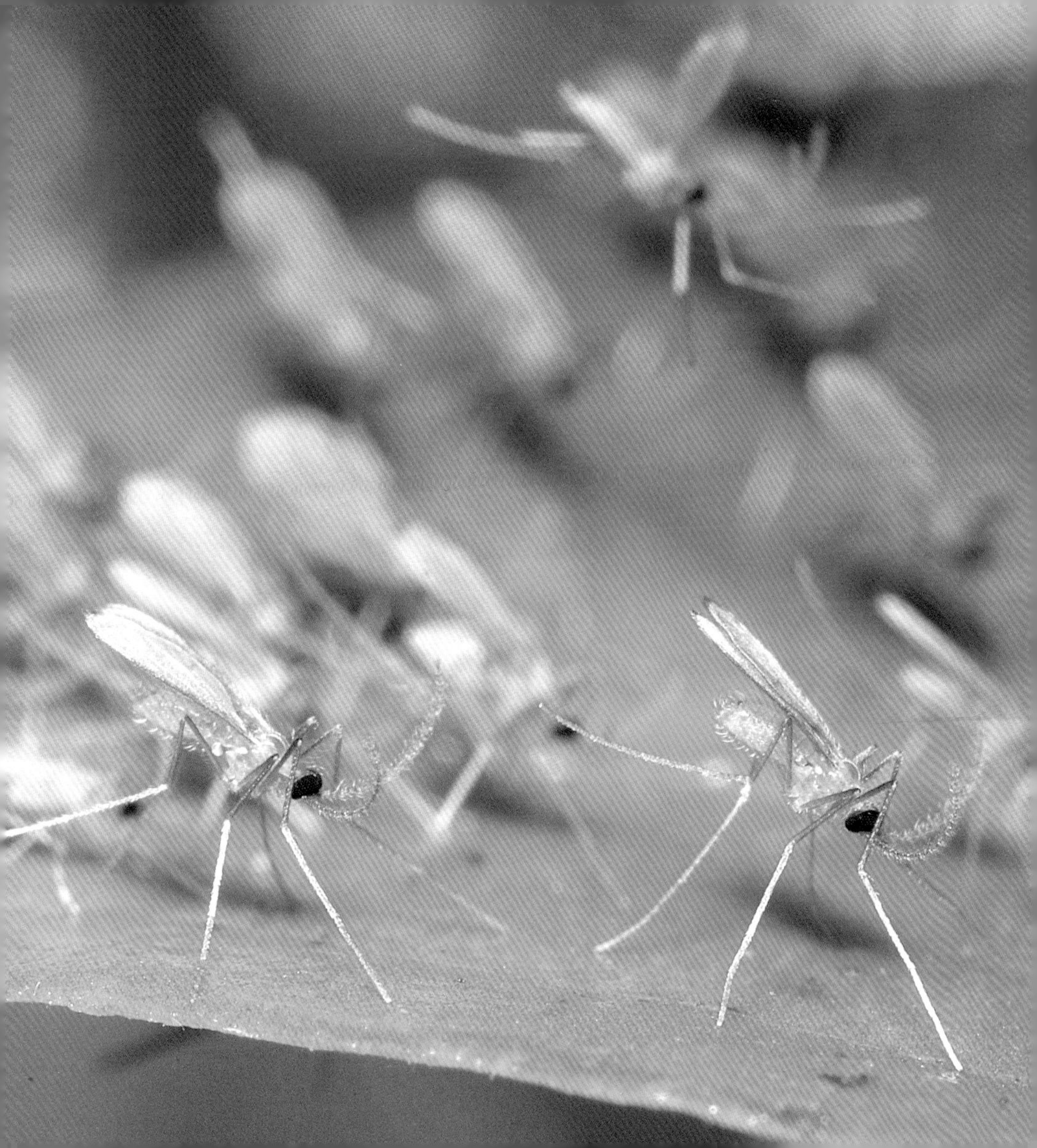

# Contents

# Introduction

Insects are overwhelmingly diverse ... so diverse you might well think it impossible to routinely recognize bugs, beetles and flies the way we expect at least a passing familiarity with most of the birds, mammals and other vertebrates that cross our paths. That perception is grounded in reality, since most known species of living things—about a million of the 1.7 million or so named species—are insects, and the number of insect species as yet undiscovered and unnamed undoubtedly runs into further millions. It all seems hopelessly overwhelming ... but it shouldn't.

Insect diversity, especially the almost untapped diversity of little-studied insects such as tiny tropical flies, should be seen as a rich ore of insights to be mined for generations to come rather than as a barrier to the study of insect natural history today. In fact, most insects are relatively easy to identify to a meaningful level. The orders of insects—the big groups such as flies, beetles, dragonflies and wasps—are few and easy to learn, and most insect species (indeed, most animal species) belong to one of only four easily recognizable orders: flies (Diptera), wasps (Hymenoptera), beetles (Coleoptera) and moths and butterflies (Lepidoptera). These orders in turn are divided into families—such as fireflies, mosquitoes and lady beetles—most of which occur worldwide and are readily recognizable anywhere on the planet as variations on familiar themes. Many of the images in this book are from "exotic" places, but most should be easily recognizable as members of familiar families that probably occur in your own backyard, even though a disproportionate number of the species shown belong to rare families or families with unusually restricted distributions. Identification beyond the family level can be more difficult, and for many groups it has traditionally been the realm of specialists with microscopes, extensive libraries and reference collections. That is changing quickly; for more and more groups and more and more regions, identification right down to genus and species is getting easier, thanks largely to the digital revolution.

If you know the family to which an insect belongs, you can make generalizations about how it lives and what it eats, but more detailed information about insect distribution and behavior is often tied to generic (genus) or specific (species) names. In general, insects from temperate

Army ants (*Eciton burchelii*) carrying a scorpion's tail in Costa Rica.

countries do have species names, and you can find the names for the most commonly encountered or distinctive species by using recent photographic guides. Identification of tropical insects is more daunting because of the huge numbers of undocumented species and a lack of published identification guides. Even in the tropics, however, many of the large and more conspicuous groups are remarkably well-known, and commonly encountered species are often easily identifiable. By way of illustration, most of the Bolivian insects illustrated in this book were photographed while I was instructing at a field course in primary rainforest near the Peruvian border. We were able to identify most of the more conspicuous insects encountered during that course through the use of a small photographic guide called *Amazon Insects* (Castner, 2000) illustrated with about 160 photographs from the Peruvian Amazon. More remarkably, during less than two weeks in the Bolivian rainforest we encountered most of the insect groups illustrated by Castner. This is not to say that either the photos in Castner's book or the 300 or so neotropical insects illustrated here represent a significant proportion of the millions of insect species thought to occur in the Amazonian rainforest, but it does suggest that they represent a meaningful proportion of the distinct kinds of larger insects an ecotourist might encounter during a visit to the South American rainforest. Similarly, the 80 or so species illustrated here from Costa Rica hardly scratch the surface of the insect diversity of that hyperdiverse Central

American country, but if you go bugwatching in Costa Rica you will probably find significant similarity between the species shown and discussed here and the insects you spot along forest trails and margins.

The photographs in this book were identified partly by using reference collections, paper guides and websites, but many of the images were identifiable only with the help of specialists—professional taxonomists who have identified hundreds of my specimens and images over the past several years. Some kinds of insects, as I have noted, are so poorly known that several of the images here are of undescribed (new) species photographed for the first time. A few of the photographs in this book are identified only to the family level because I could not identify them further, nor could I find a specialist able to identify them for me. An enormous amount of basic taxonomy remains to be completed before tropical insects will be covered by accessible identification tools like the wonderful guides now appearing for many groups of insects in temperate countries.

Although this book will undoubtedly find use as a tool for identifying naturalists' digital images from bugwatching excursions near and far, it was not assembled as an identification guide, and it provides neither comprehensive coverage for any region nor balanced coverage across the Insecta. Instead, it is a compilation of images that illustrate insect diversity, form and function around the world. Most of the examples are drawn from the neotropics—Earth's major cauldron of diversity—but a few are from other areas, including Australia, New Zealand, temperate South America, the Pacific, the Caribbean and North America.

## Insect Distributions

Since the images in this book were taken in lands scattered across half the planet, some comments on why which insects live where might be in order. If you check out the insects in your backyard or a city park, most of the species you encounter are likely to be secondarily widespread creatures that have travelled around the planet thanks to mankind's deliberate or accidental intervention. Ask a friend to name ten kinds of insects and I will bet that eight of them are European or Asian species that are now common in much of the world: European Earwigs, Cabbage White Butterflies, House Flies, most cockroaches, most crop pests, most common lady beetles, most common ground beetles, common hornets, yellowjackets and paper wasps—the list goes on and on, as does the stream of new invaders arriving on foreign shores to displace native species. A few such invaders are included here, but most of the insects on the following pages were photographed in native ranges that still reflect the pre-human history of the planet, ranges that are Earth's collective memory of origins, expansions, divisions and contractions of habitats. Hundreds of millions of years of planetary change have divided, subdivided, recombined and divided species ranges again and again, driving speciation and generating the biodiversity that defines life on Earth today.

When you look at a picture of an insect from an exotic place, try to think of where you have seen something similar. The odds are that the similarity you see reflects relationship, and that the insect belongs to a recognizable genus, a familiar family or at least a known order. At some point in the near or distant past that exotic insect shared a common ancestor with something you know. That bug from Cuba, for example, might have a very close relative in the American southeast, and those two species in turn might be very similar to a member of the same genus in northeastern North America. Related species are often similar because they resemble a common ancestor that was somehow subdivided—perhaps by a barrier such as a mountain range or body of water—into populations that evolved into different species. Professional taxonomists routinely plot phylogenies (like genealogies that show the relationship between species rather than individuals) of groups of related species against the geographic distribution of the species, and in doing so often show neat matches between the divisions in

**A Costa Rican mantisfly (*Zeugomantispa compellens*) freshly emerged from a spider egg case.**

the phylogenetic trees and the divisions between areas or patches of habitat. Generally, the more distant the relationship between exotic insects and those you know, the longer they have been separated. Thus, some insects from Central America look much like exotic versions of North American species with which they share a relatively recent common history, while Australian or Chilean insects are, in contrast, often strikingly different from the insect groups familiar to most North Americans and Europeans.

One of the terms frequently used in this book is the term *endemism* (or *endemic*). An endemic species is a species that originated in an area and still occurs there; for example, the termites illustrated on page 54 are found on Robinson Crusoe Island (one of the Juan Fernandez Islands of Chile) and nowhere else, and are thus endemic to one island. Islands typically have very high endemism, as do other isolated areas such as mountaintops. Australia and Chile are examples of countries with very high endemism because of their isolation from other countries where related insects occur—Australia because it is an ancient island, and Chile because it is bounded by water to the west and south, mountains to the east and desert to the north.

## Collecting and Photographing Insects

The study of insects in the field—let's call it bugwatching, since it has much in common with the more limited hobby of birdwatching—usually involves capturing a specimen or image for study, identification and permanent record. The traditional approach to insect study has been to capture and kill specimens, usually preserving them as dried exoskeletons impaled on pins, and later identifying them by using a hand lens or microscope to examine morphological details described in printed keys or identification guides. This apparently anachronistic approach is still necessary for serious specimen-based studies of insect systematics, but bugwatching as a natural-history pursuit is enjoying an overdue resurgence of popularity because it is now possible to go out and "capture" specimens with digital cameras and assemble a digital collection without killing anything, and without the hassle of getting collecting permits, poisons, pins, labels, storage boxes and the other paraphernalia of the professional entomologist. Furthermore, it is now possible to identify an ever-increasing range of insects merely by matching your digital images to similarly shaped and colored images in recent books and on the Web. This is not to suggest that the millions of insect species out there can all be identified by color and shape, but an impressive proportion of those you are likely to digitally collect are distinctive and can be recognized from good images.

Good images of insects down to mosquito size and even below can be obtained with most digital cameras, or even your cell phone, with a bit of practice and a lot of patience. The trick to insect photography is to get to know your subjects and to approach them slowly; whether you then shoot them with a pocket "point-and-shoot" or a fancy digital SLR (single-lens reflex) camera is unimportant. Excellent images for Web-posting or developing a digital insect collection can be obtained using pocket cameras, but the images for this book were taken with larger SLR cameras. A few were taken using film cameras equipped with macro lenses and flash units, but most were taken with the same lenses on newer digital SLR bodies.

## Basic Bug Biology

The pictures in this book usually show adult insects, but bear in mind that most insects have fascinating life cycles that include wingless immature and winged adult stages. Everybody is familiar with the life cycle of a butterfly: it starts with an egg that hatches into a wingless larva (caterpillar), then transforms into a pupal stage that later undergoes another metamorphic molt to the familiar butterfly stage. This kind of development, called complete metamorphosis, characterizes most members of the big, familiar orders (beetles, flies, wasps, moths) and many smaller ones, but even within these orders there are lots of variations on the theme. Loss of wings, for example, is common (ants and fleas, of course, but also wingless flies, beetles and even wingless moths), and several groups bypass the egg stage. Not all insects undergo complete metamorphosis; many orders of more "primitive" winged insects hatch from eggs not as wingless larvae, but as nymphs with small wing buds that later burst into complete wings without the need for a pupal stage. Grasshoppers, dragonflies, mayflies and true bugs experience this kind of development. A few, still more primitive insects predate the origin of wings; in their simple development each successive stage looks like the one before. The stages in an insect's development are made necessary by its external skeleton, which is like a suit of armor that has to be periodically discarded and replaced with a bigger one as the insect grows. These stages, or instars, are punctuated by molting, or casting of the old skin, which is soon replaced by a new and larger exoskeleton.

## Basic Bug Structure

This book is restricted to the class Insecta, a special group of invertebrates with certain defining attributes. They have an external skeleton and jointed appendages, which puts them in the phylum Arthropoda, but they differ from other arthropods in having a single pair of antennae, a pair of (generally) chewing mouthparts called mandibles, and—most important—six legs. The body is divided into a head, a thorax and an abdomen that usually lacks appendages other than those involved in mating and laying eggs. The thorax is the muscle-packed section that supports the legs and—usually, and unlike all other invertebrates—one or two pairs of wings, while the head is modified characteristically in each order of insects. The mouthparts of beetles, grasshoppers, wasps and many other insects adhere to the basic design of chunky chewing mandibles followed by segmented maxillae that help in food manipulation, but those of moths, flies and true bugs are much modified, with missing or inconspicuous mandibles. Moth mouthparts are usually dominated by a coiled, straw-like proboscis, most flies have sponge-like mouthparts, and true bugs pierce their food with hypodermic syringes made of slender drawn-out mandibles and maxillae.

## The Ins and Outs (and -inis and -inaes) of Taxonomic Names

The class Insecta is divided into orders, which are mostly big, familiar groups such as Lepidoptera (butterflies and moths), Diptera (flies) and Coleoptera (beetles). There are no standard endings for order names, but they often end in *-ptera*, which is Greek for "wing." Lepidoptera translates as "scaly wing," Diptera translates as "two wing" and Coleoptera translates as "sheath wing." Orders are divided into families, and family-level identification is the secret to appreciating the world of insects—which is a good thing, since it is often difficult to identify them beyond the family level. You can always recognize a family name by the ending *-idae*; for example, Muscidae is the House Fly family and Carabidae is the ground beetle family. Larger families are often divided into subfamilies, and the subfamily level can be very useful in large groups such as the Scarabaeidae (scarab beetles). You can always recognize a subfamily name by the ending *-inae*, as in Rutelinae (the shining leaf chafer subfamily). In a few groups the subfamilies are further divided into tribes, which are always given names ending in *-ini*. Subfamilies and tribes are given here only where they are of special interest.

All species are grouped into genera, and species names are always given in combination with the generic name; for example, *Acromyrmex versicolor* is a Southwestern American species in the genus *Acromyrmex*. In a scientific work it is proper form to cite the author of a species following the first use of the species name, so if this were a scientific work the correct way to refer to the Desert Leafcutting Ant would be *Acromyrmex versicolor* (Pergande), since Pergande named this species (his name is in brackets to indicate that he originally described the species in a different genus). Since this is not really a scientific work, I have excluded author names to make the text a bit more readable. Generic and species names are always in italics, with the genus name (but never the species name) capitalized. Formal common names that refer to a single species are always capitalized, as are formal scientific names for families, tribes, subfamilies and orders. Thus we have the Desert Leafcutting Ant (*Acromyrmex versicolor*), a common species in the genus *Acromyrmex* in the tribe Attini (leafcutting ants) of the subfamily Myrmicinae (a group of stinging ants including fire ants and leafcutting ants) in the family Formicidae (all ants) in the order Hymenoptera.

**Desert Leafcutting Ant (*Acromyrmex versicolor*) from southern California.**

# Water Springtail

These were among the thousands of tiny Water Springtails, *Podura aquatica*, clustered on the surface of an eastern Canadian pond. Several springtail species occur on the surfaces of ponds, puddles and lakes, where they scavenge pollen and other material that falls onto the water surface. The Water Springtail, one of only four living species in the ancient family Poduridae, is able to jump off the water surface by using a conspicuously long and flattened "springtail." Springtails (order Collembola, sometimes treated as a separate class) make up an ancient lineage that may be more closely related to crustaceans than to true insects.

# Elongate Springtail

This distinctive elongate springtail (family Entomobryidae) was photographed on debris brushed from shoreline litter into a South Carolina creek. Soil and leaf litter always abound in springtails, which often reach densities of over a thousand per cubic yard. This individual belongs to the worldwide but mostly tropical genus *Salina*. Springtails (order Collembola) are among the oldest animal lineages; their fossils date back about 400 million years.

# Globular Springtail

Springtails (order Collembola) are easily overlooked because of their lilliputian scale (only a few millimeters in length), but these ubiquitous little arthropods are so colorful and diverse they deserve to be admired as the butterflies of the microarthropod world. That is especially true for the roly-poly members of the globular springtail suborder, such as this *Ptenothrix atra* (family Dicyrtomidae) photographed in some Canadian leaf litter.

# Giant Springtail

Most springtails are minute and easily overlooked, but some of the so-called giant springtails of New Zealand can reach the whopping length of almost 0.8 inch (2 cm). This New Zealand springtail (*Holacanthella brevispinosa*) is a relatively small representative of the giant springtail group (family Neanuridae).

# Jumping Bristletail

Jumping bristletails (order Archaeognatha) make up an ancient lineage of robust wingless insects covered with colored scales much like those found on butterflies and moths. Although rarely noticed and poorly known, jumping bristletails are widespread in habitats ranging from deserts to seashores. One of the species shown here is running across the open sand on a desert flat in Arizona; another is scurrying along a twig on the floor of an Arizona oak forest (inset).

# Mayfly

Mayflies (order Ephemeroptera) are unique among winged insects in having two winged stages, of which the first (the winged subimago or subadult stage shown here) is a sort of evolutionary appendix retained only in the mayflies (no other insect continues to grow and molt once it is fully winged). The aquatic nymphs of mayflies leave the water to transform into milky-winged subimagos that usually fly away from the water to transform into clear-winged adults. Males of some mayflies, such as this baetid (family Baetidae) subimago, have greatly enlarged eyes that probably help them maintain position in mating swarms.

# Hendrickson Mayfly

The big-eyed male of this pair of eastern North American Hendrickson Mayflies (*Ephemerella subvaria*) has used his ultra-long front legs to assist in "docking" under a small-eyed female. Mayfly mating usually takes place in the air, but this pair settled briefly to the ground before the female left to release a mass of eggs into a nearby river. The leaf-gilled nymphs in this family (Ephemerellidae) are known as spiny crawlers (inset).

# Rainbow Bluet



The colorful male of this pair of damselflies (Rainbow Bluets, *Enallagma antennatum*), seen along the edge of a slow-moving Ontario stream, has gripped the female just behind her head, using a pair of appendages at the tip of his abdomen. The female will later loop the tip of her abdomen forward to pick up some sperm the male previously deposited in the secondary copulatory organ near the front of his abdomen.

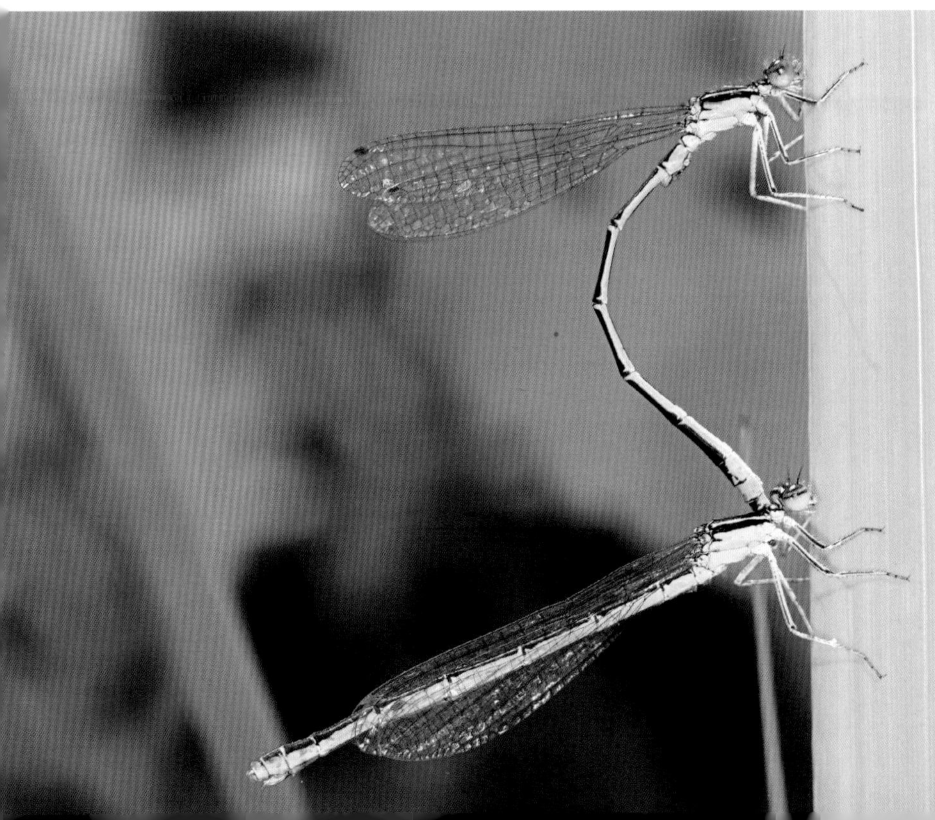

# Thule Bluet

Bluets (genus *Enallagma*, family Coenagrionidae) are the most common damselflies in North America, and they can often be seen inserting their eggs into plant stems submerged in lakes and slow-moving streams. After mating, males of these Thule Bluets (*E. carunculatum*) use their abdominal claspers to hang on to the front of the female's thorax, guarding her from other males as she lays eggs.

# Eastern Forktail Damselfly



This damselfly (Eastern Forktail, *Ischnura verticalis*, family Coenagrionidae) is laying her eggs by lowering her abdomen into a weedy Ontario pond, probably inserting the tip of her abdomen into a stem of an aquatic plant. Some damselfly females go right underwater to lay eggs, often accompanied by a male that maintains his grip on her thorax, guarding her from other males throughout the whole process.

ODONATA

# Eastern Forktail Damselfly

This adult forktail damselfly (*Ischnura*, family Coenagrionidae) has just emerged from its nymphal skin in an algae-choked pond. Its wings are not yet inflated, so they look like wrinkled stubs. Damselflies, including this one, often carry numerous parasitic mites (*Arrenurus* spp.) that crawl from aquatic damselfly nymphs onto the newly terrestrial adults such as this one. The mites then pierce the adult damselflies with their mouthparts.

# Tropical Rockmaster Damselfly

This robust Australian damselfly belongs to an ancient, mostly tropical, lineage (family Amphipterygidae or family Lestoideidae), including about 20 species of robust, dragonfly-like damselflies. *Diphlebia euphoeoides* lays its eggs in the rivers of eastern Australian rainforests, where they hatch into tuft-gilled nymphs able to survive in seasonally dried-up river beds.

# Dragonfly and Damselfly

Damselfly and dragonfly nymphs have a remarkable lower lip (labium) that is hinged at the middle and ends in a pair of jagged-toothed lobes (palpi). To envisage how damselflies and dragonflies grab prey, put the palm of your hand over your mouth and tuck your elbow against your chest. Now shoot your hand out to grab a snack and pull it back to your mouth in a fraction of a second, and you will have the idea, although dragonflies and damselflies use hydraulic pressure to shoot their lower lip out in lightning-fast strikes. These images show the robust head of a spiketail dragonfly nymph (*Cordulegaster*, family Cordulegastridae, inset) and the slender, elongate-lipped nymph of a spreadwing damselfly (*Lestes*, family Lestidae).

# Helicopter Damselfly

The giant "helicopter damselflies" (family Pseudostigmatidae) of Central and South America are among the world's most spectacular insects, and seeing them hover over a spider web to snatch an eight-legged snack is always a thrill. Males of *Microstigma rotundatum* have yellow wing spots (inset) and females have white wing spots; this female is laying eggs in a rain-filled hole in a decaying log beside a Bolivian rainforest trail. The predaceous nymphs will feed on mosquito larvae and other insects in the tree hole.

# Common Whitetail

The Common Whitetail (*Libellula lydia*) is a familiar dragonfly across North America, where it breeds in a wide variety of waters ranging from polluted urban streams to pristine marshes. Males such as this one are territorial, challenging interloping males by raising their brilliant white abdomen in a threat display. Females, like those of other skimmer dragonflies (family Libellulidae), are often seen skimming the water surface as they deposit their eggs.

# Calico Pennant

This bright red male Calico Pennant (*Celithemis elisa*, family Libellulidae) is watching for prey and potential mates from a prominent perch atop the dead stem of a pondside weed. Females, such as this one perching on the side of a stem (inset), are much more subdued in color. After mating, the female will skim along a pond surface to release her eggs.

# Amazonian Amberwing Dragonfly

Dragonflies in the family Libellulidae are sometimes called skimmers because of their habit of skimming along the water surface to drop their eggs; they are also sometimes called perchers because of their characteristic resting pose. This tiny *Perithemis thais* is perching on a twig over a muddy Amazonian stream.

# Band-winged Meadowhawk



These Band-winged Meadowhawks (*Sympetrum semicinctum*, family Libellulidae) are mating in a northern Ontario fen, where they developed from nymphs in shallow, weedy pools. Prior to mating the male deposited sperm (produced at the tip of his abdomen) in what amounts to an extra penis (a "secondary copulatory organ") on the underside of the body just behind the thorax; here he is using the tip of his abdomen to grip his mate behind her head as she arcs her abdomen forward to reach his secondary copulatory organ.

# Skimmer Dragonfly

Dragonfly nymphs such as these skimmers (family Libellulidae) are predators that grab prey with a long, hinged lower lip. The end of the lower lip (labium), which has jagged-toothed grasping lobes (palpi), usually sits cup-like under the head, but the base of the lip is long and hinged in the middle, and it can be extended in a fraction of a second. One of these images shows the head of a skimmer nymph at rest; the other (inset) shows a nymph with its lower lip extended.

# Darner Dragonfly

Nymphs of darner dragonflies (family Aeshnidae) have a long, hinged grasping lower lip normally held flat under the head. It can be swiftly extended to grab prey such as the small fish being held and consumed by one of the darner nymphs shown here. The big dragonflies called mosquito hawks or devil's darning needles are in this group. The former name is accurate, since they scoop up huge numbers of mosquitoes, but the latter name reflects an old folk tale that darners use their long abdomens to sew up the lips of liars.

# Baskettail Dragonfly

This baskettail dragonfly nymph (*Epitheca*, family Corduliidae) is clinging to a pondside stem as it molts to the adult stage, which seems to be exploding from a split in the back of the nymphal skin. The inset shows the same adult resting above the nymphal skin a few minutes later, with its wings fully inflated but not yet fully hardened and ready for flight.

# Green Darner



Dragonflies, such as this Green Darner (*Anax junius*, family Aeshnidae), have insignificant little antennae, and they clearly rely on their massive eyes for spotting winged prey. Flying insects are scooped up in the bristly basket made up of the dragonfly's long hind legs, shorter mid legs and shortest front legs; captured insects are then masticated by a pair of massive mandibles underneath the dragonfly's head. The Green Darner is one of the few migratory North American dragonflies. Some (but not all) Green Darners leave the northern United States and southern Canada each fall to fly to points unknown in the southern U.S., the Caribbean or Mexico.

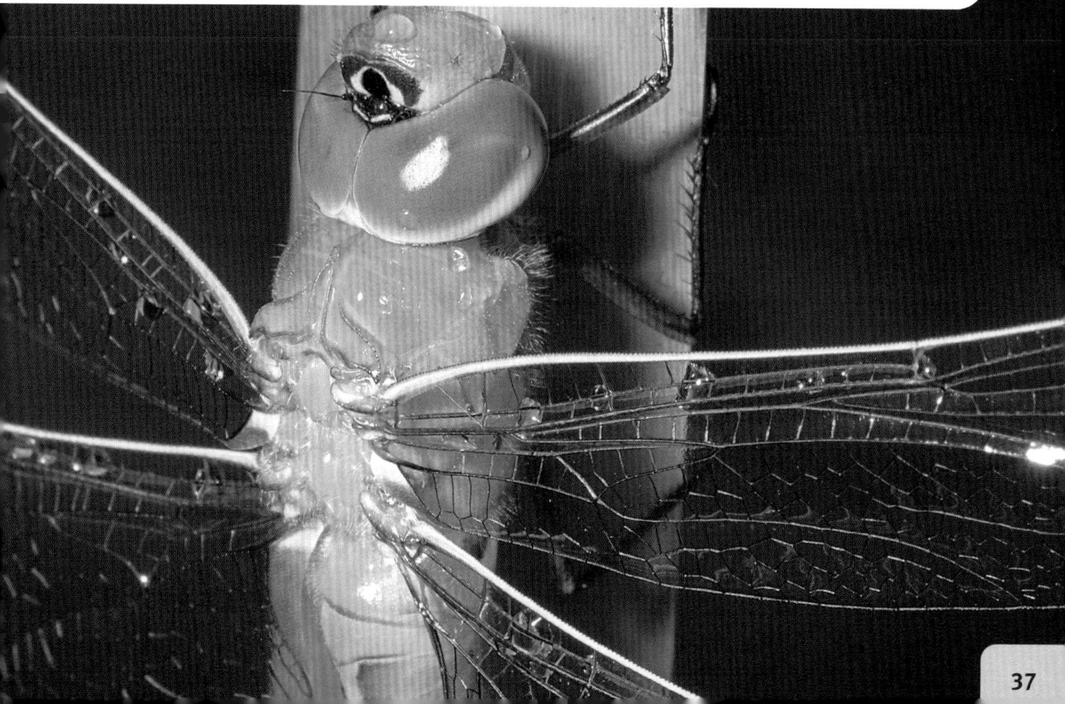

# Petaltail Dragonfly

Petaltails (family Petaluridae), such as this *Uropetala carovei* from New Zealand, are among the most ancient of all winged insects, with fossils dating back to the Jurassic period (around 150 million years ago). The name "petaltail" refers to the broad anal appendages you can see at the tip of this male's abdomen, but females are more interesting for their habit of hovering over mossy banks, darting in periodically to stick an egg in the moss. Petaltail nymphs dig burrows from which they strike out at passing terrestrial insects—an unusual strategy for a dragonfly nymph, but remarkably like the feeding strategy of tiger beetle larvae.

# Apache Spiketail Dragonfly



Female spiketails (family Cordulegastridae) have a spike-like adominal tip used to drive eggs into the bottoms or banks of streams or seepages. This Apache Spiketail (*Cordulegaster diadema*) is exhibiting a typical pose for a perching spiketail as it clings to a twig at an oblique angle. This photo is from Arizona, but the Apache Spiketail ranges from the American southwest to Central America.

# Sulphur-tipped Clubtail Dragonfly

Clubtails, such as this Sulphur-tipped Clubtail (*Gomphus militaris*) from New Mexico, often have a swollen, or "clubbed," abdomen. Nymphs usually ambush prey from the cover of debris at the bottom of streams; adults often perch on the ground, but this one was perching horizontally a couple of yards above the sizzling soil surface in the Chihuahuan desert.

# Stonefly



This green stonefly (Chloroperlidae) has just transformed from the nymphal to the adult stage; the cast skin of the aquatic nymph can be seen clinging to the streamside stem under the body of the soft, pale new adult. The adult will harden up a bit and attain its mature green color before mating and laying eggs back in the river from which the nymph emerged.

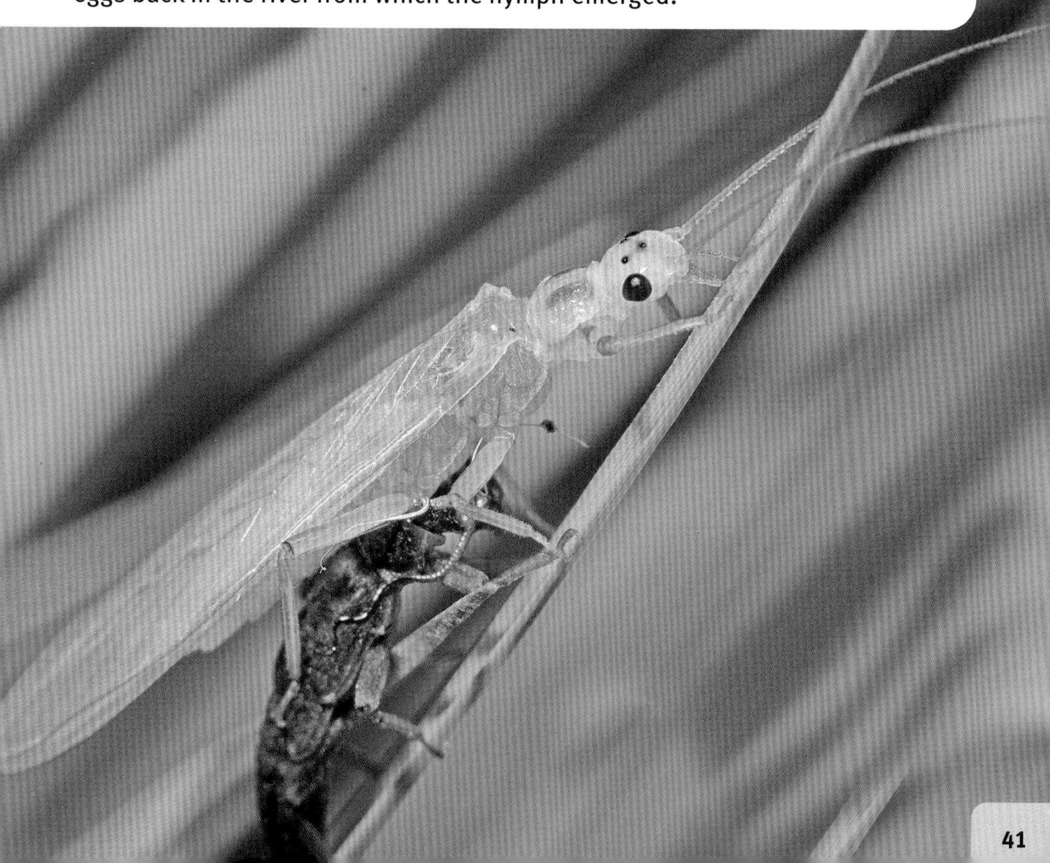

# Stonefly

This summer stonefly (Perlidae) nymph has just cast its skin to allow growth to the next nymphal stage, and the newly molted nymph is soft, pale and vulnerable. Soon it will harden and darken into a predaceous nymph that will eat other insect inhabitants of its swiftly flowing river home.

# Stonefly

Stonefly adults (order Plecoptera), as the name suggests, are often found on stones or other objects near the running water in which they develop as nymphs. This 2-inch-long stonefly was photographed on a wall near a Chilean stream in 2006 and it remains the only specimen ever seen of the species *Diamphipnoa colberti* (family Diamphipnoidae). Stonefly expert William Stark named the species in 2008 on the basis of this individual, coining the species name to honor a favorite American comedian.

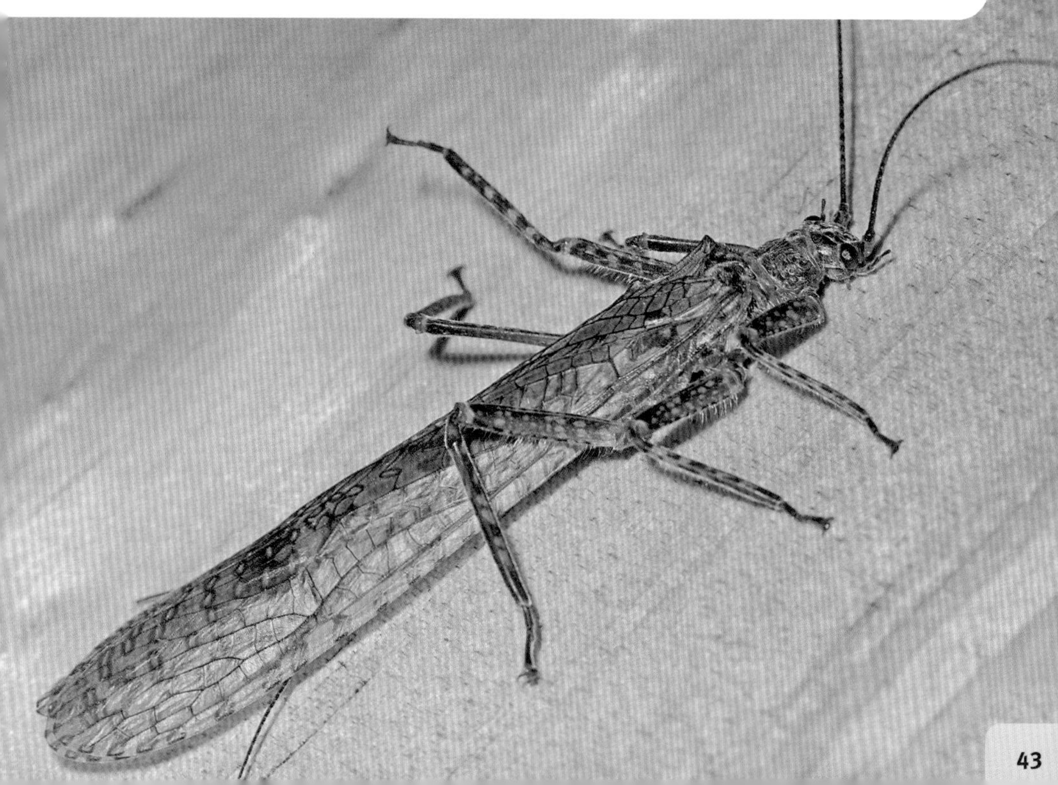

# Earwig

Earwigs (order Dermaptera) are easily recognized by the stout, curved, forceps-like cerci at the end of the abdomen. The cerci are used for mating, tucking the hind wings away under the short forewings, prey capture and defense. Their effectiveness as weapons is augmented by defensive sprays produced at the base of the abdomen. In the few species studied in detail, the openings of these glands are always aimed at the base of the cerci, so whatever the earwig pinches is on target for a nasty chemical squirt. This is a *Carcinophora* (family Anisolabidae) from Costa Rica.

# Earwig

This Bolivian earwig (*Pyragra fuscata*) belongs to one of the most "primitive" groups of living earwigs, the family Pygidicranidae. Members of this family are known from Cretaceous amber fossils from Myanmar ("Burmese amber"), the oldest known fossils of a living earwig family. The earwig order, Dermaptera, is very old, with fossils of extinct families reflecting a history extending back to the late Triassic period, more than 200 million years ago.

# Earwig

Earwigs such as this *Spongiphora buprestoides* from Bolivia (family Labiidae) make up a relatively small order (Dermaptera) of just under 2,000 species. Although the life histories of most species remain unknown, many earwigs are commonly found under bark and in leaf litter. A few omnivorous species are minor pests; females of all species probably guard and groom their eggs and newly hatched nymphs. This Striped Earwig (*Labidura riparia*, family Labiduridae, inset), photographed along the muddy shore of the Salton Sea in California, is a cosmopolitan species reported as capturing a variety of prey insects with its forceps-like cerci.

# Carolina Mantis

Mantids (order Mantodea) are a mostly tropical group, and the Carolina Mantis (*Stagmomantis carolina*) is one of the few native species found in temperate North America. This is one of the mantis species that sometimes exhibits sexual cannibalism. In about a quarter of mating encounters the female eats the male, starting with the head and continuing along the thorax while his abdomen continues to move and he carries on fertilizing her eggs.

# Hooded Mantid

Hooded mantids, such as this *Choeradodis rhombicollis* from Costa Rica, are especially inconspicuous among tropical foliage because of their greatly expanded pronotum (the top of the first thoracic segment). Other mantid species look like blades of grass, sticks, bark, flowers and stones; some species in Africa and Australia can even turn black after a fire to blend in with the burned background. All 2,300 species of the order Mantodea (most are in the family Mantidae) are predators.

# Mantid



This Bolivian mantid (*Callibia diana*) is conspicuous on the surface of a leaf, but it would be well camouflaged on the mottled surface of a fungus-spotted branch of a rainforest tree. Mantids (order Mantodea, mostly family Mantidae) are easy to identify by their grasping (raptorial) front legs and big-eyed, almost triangular head. Many mantids, like these small nymphs from Costa Rica (inset), forego camouflage for mimicry in their early stages, and deter predators by their behavioral and morphological similarity to ants.

# Cockroach

Although almost everyone is familiar with the few widespread pest species of cockroaches (order Blattodea), most roaches are innocuous tropical insects, and most parts of the world abound in interesting native roaches. Australia, for example, has 430 or so species of roaches, including many wingless "bush cockroaches" (family Blattidae) such as this one from Western Australia, as well as winged species such as these mating *Balta* (family Blatellidae) from Queensland.

# Madagascar Hissing Cockroach

The Madagascar Hissing Cockroach (*Gromphadorhina portentosa*, family Blaberidae), originally from Madagascar, is now a popular pet because of its large size (2–3 inches/5–7.6 cm), longevity (five years or so), ease of culture and remarkable habit of "hissing" loudly by forcing air through the abdominal breathing pores (spiracles). All mature hissing cockroaches can hiss, but the males take it to an extreme, using it as a challenge during fights with other male roaches. Unlike familiar domestic roach species such as the German Cockroach, hissing roaches carry their egg case internally until the eggs have hatched. Like wingless wood roaches found in North America and elsewhere, hissing roach nymphs and adults stay in family groups for long periods.

# Peppered Roach

The head of this Peppered Roach (*Archimandrita tesselata*, family Blaberidae) is completely concealed under the broad, shield-like top of the first segment of the thorax (the pronotum). Cockroach culturing is now a growing hobby, and these long-lived and massive (about 3 inches/7.6 cm) roaches are favored by hobbyists because they neither fly nor climb up the glass walls of their indoor habitats. This one was photographed “in the wild” in a Costa Rican rainforest.

# Cockroach



Many cockroaches remain wingless or short-winged throughout their lives. This flightless Bolivian roach (family Blatellidae), flushed from under the bark of a dead tree, made up for its inability to fly by running with impressive speed. Most of the 4,000 or so world species live in the tropics. Cockroaches are usually omnivores, but a few (like the very closely related termites) eat wood that they digest with the aid of symbiotic microorganisms.

# Robinson Crusoe Termite

All termites are social insects that live in colonies made up mostly of hundreds to thousands of wingless workers that do not reproduce. The winged individuals among these *Kalotermes* (*Neotermes*) *gracilignathus* (family Kalotermitidae) on Robinson Crusoe Island are males and females about to take a mating flight. Once mated, a male and a female (the "king" and "queen") will break off their wings and start a new colony.

# Nailhead Termite

The insects known throughout the Caribbean as "nailheads" are the soldiers of nasutiform termites (order Isoptera, family Termitidae)—pointy-headed insects able to use their nozzle-like noses to squirt caustic glue onto attacking ants and other enemies. These are the common termites that make covered tunnels along tree trunks that often lead to conspicuous brown carton-like nests. If you break a tunnel to expose a column of workers, the distinctive nozzle-headed soldiers will soon appear.

# Nailhead Termite

The big, fat termite surrounded by small, pointy-headed soldiers and a few pale workers is a queen nasutiform termite exposed by breaking open a Bolivian carton nest. Queen termites establish colonies after a single mating flight, later growing into massive, long-lived egg-laying machines. Termites, traditionally treated as the order Isoptera, are now treated as part of the cockroach order (Blattodea).

# Nailhead Termite

Some of the most colorful termites of neotropical rainforests also make some of the most attractive nests (right). These Bolivian *Constrictotermes* termites (family Termitidae) are dark brown and orange, and their carton-like nests are elegantly sculptured. Like other nasutiform termites, their soldiers have pointy heads that serve as glue-squirting defensive weapons able to gum up the antennae of enemy ants.

# Syntermes Termite

This column of Bolivian termites (*Syntermes* sp., family Termitidae) disappeared into a hole in the ground moments after this photograph was taken, but not before a bystander tested the defensive ability of the soldier termites standing guard over the column. As you can see from the impaled finger (inset), the soldier's wicked-looking mandibles are indeed sharp and effective defensive weapons.

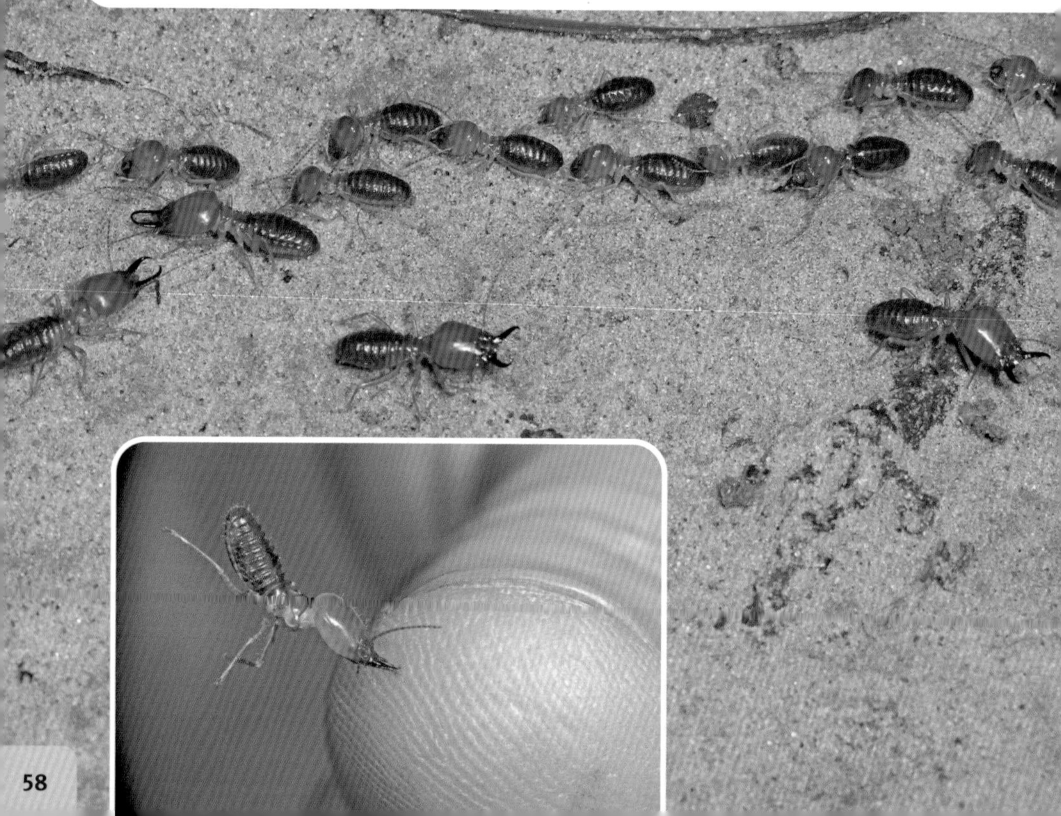

# Stick Insect

Stick insects (order Phasmatodea) are aptly named for their stick-like camouflage, which renders these slender, slow-moving and cryptically colored insects virtually invisible in their native habitat. These images show a skinny brown Australian male stick insect and his fat mate (right), plus a very well concealed couple of green New Zealand stick insects.

# Stick Insect

The world's longest insects are stick insects or walkingsticks (order Phasmatodea)—the record-holding species (from Malaysia) reaching an astonishing 22 inches (55.5 cm). The much smaller but still impressive species shown here on my son's back was knocked from a tree branch in Costa Rica, where it was all but invisible among the lichen-spattered twigs.

# Handsome Trig Bush Cricket



This Handsome Trig or Red-headed Bush Cricket (*Phyllopalpus pulchellus*), photographed in North Carolina, is a distinctive member of the cricket subfamily Trigonidiinae (family Gryllidae). The club-like structures held out in front of the head are mouthpart lobes called palpi (*Phyllopalpus* translates as "leaf palpus"). Male Handsome Trigs, like other male crickets, sing to attract females by rubbing their forewings together; unlike most crickets, this brightly colored species sings during the day.

# Jerusalem Cricket

The "Jerusalem crickets" of western North America (mostly in the genus *Stenopelmatus*) are neither crickets nor from Jerusalem, but are instead members of a group (family Stenopelmatidae) that includes the giant wetas of New Zealand and the king crickets of Australia. These charmingly big-headed insects lack both wings and ears but nonetheless "sing" by beating the abdomen against the ground; they "hear" the song as vibrations transmitted through the ground. Like true crickets, they are omnivores that eat other insects or dead organic material.

# Colored Cricket



The "Grillo Colorado" or colored cricket (*Cratomelus* sp.) of Chile is in the same group (Stenopelmatidae) as the giant wetas and tree wetas of New Zealand and the king crickets of Australia. These flightless, night-active insects are commonly encountered under logs. Some members of this group are enormous, and a New Zealand species is probably the world's heaviest insect (about 2.5 ounces/70 g).

# Japanese Burrowing Cricket

Raising crickets is a traditional Chinese hobby dating back more than a thousand years, and it is still important in some parts of China where crickets are raised both as singers and fighters. Cricket fighting remains an enormously popular (albeit generally illegal) activity, often linked to substantial wagers. This stout cricket is a *Velarifictorus micado*, the species most often reared and sold as a *cu zhi* (fighting cricket) in China, where prize crickets sometimes sell for more than a thousand dollars. In North America, where the species has recently been introduced and is spreading through the east, it is known as the Japanese Burrowing Cricket.

# False Leaf Katydid

This Costa Rican long-horned grasshopper (family Tettigoniidae) must have fallen from the foliage, where it would have been superbly camouflaged, to the leaf litter, where it was easily spotted. Like crickets, long-horned grasshoppers usually have species-specific songs, and closely related species sometimes differ only in the details of the stridulatory apparatus (the file and scraper used for singing) and the song. This is probably *Orophus tessellatus*, a false leaf katydid of the forest understory, but it is almost identical to *O. conspersus*, which is common in more disturbed habitats.

# Collared Katydid

This brightly colored Bolivian katydid (*Euceraia* sp., family Tettigoniidae) is called a collared katydid because the pronotum (the area just behind the head) looks like a garish collar. Collared katydids are close relatives of the familiar green bush katydids (*Scudderia* spp.) found throughout North America. The bright color of collared katydids suggests that, unlike the camouflaged bush katydids, they are packing potent defenses against predation.

# Leaf Katydid and Lichen Katydid



Tropical grasshoppers and katydids have various ways of avoiding predation, including chemical defenses associated with warning coloration, wasp mimicry and camouflage. These two Costa Rican katydids resemble a damaged leaf and a patch of lichen. The lichen-matching species (*Markia hystrix*) is itself a voracious predator, often appearing at lights during the night, where it eats other insects attracted to the glow.

# Grasshopper

Most grasshoppers, like this sand-colored adult on a Chilean beach, are superbly camouflaged to blend in with the soil or vegetation. Most insects that stand out with contrasting colors are chemically protected or for some other reason are species that predators are well-warned to avoid. The bright pink of this Chilean grasshopper nymph probably constitutes warning (aposomatic) colors. Similar pink colors appear occasionally in several normally cryptic and presumably edible insects, including some common North American grasshoppers.

# Rainbow Grasshopper

Dry areas of the southwestern United States and Mexico abound in brightly colored and presumably inedible grasshoppers such as those in the genus *Dactylotum* (family Acrididae). This flightless Rainbow Grasshopper (*Dactylotum bicolor*) made no attempt to escape when I approached it in the Arizona desert, apparently confident in the protection advertised by its conspicuous warning coloration.

# Solanum Grasshopper

Brightly colored grasshoppers in the neotropical genus *Drymophilacris* (family Acrididae), such as this undescribed species from Costa Rica, are entirely wingless and conspicuous. However, they are rarely molested by predators because they feed on the chemically protected foliage of plants in the potato family, sequestering the plant's defensive compounds for their own use.

# Differential Grasshoppers



Differential Grasshoppers (*Melanoplus differentialis*, family Acrididae) are widespread pest grasshoppers in North America, consuming a variety of crops and sometimes occurring in outbreak numbers. After mating, this female will wiggle much of her abdomen into the ground and deposit a pod of eggs due to hatch into hungry nymphs the following spring.

# Panther-spotted Grasshopper

This Panther-spotted Grasshopper (*Poecilotettix pantherina*, family Acrididae), one of many seen in the same Arizona desert shrub, is a southwestern species ranging from New Mexico and Arizona into Mexico. Despite its apparently bright appearance it was almost invisible among the dappled foliage of its host plant.

# Snakeweed Grasshopper

The Snakeweed Grasshopper (*Hesperotettix viridis*, family Acrididae) is an abundant hopper in the American southwest but also occurs in lower numbers across the continent and north to Canada. Some of its host plants, including snakeweed, are poisonous to livestock, so Snakeweed Grasshoppers are considered beneficial insects.

# Cattail Toothpick Grasshopper

Cattail Toothpick Grasshoppers (*Leptysma marginicollis*) belong to a group aptly called the slant-faced grasshoppers, a subgroup of the family Acrididae. These two brown hoppers facing each other across a green stem were photographed in midwinter among a mixture of green and brown individuals clinging to stems in a South Carolina coastal swamp. Toothpick grasshoppers use blunt-toothed mandibles to chew away at the tough leaves of grassy plants.

# Handsome Grasshopper

The slant-faced grasshopper genus *Syrbula* (family Acrididae) includes only three species, of which the aptly named Handsome Grasshopper (*Syrbula admirabilis*, inset) is the most widespread and common. This individual was photographed in Arizona, but the same species occurs in grasslands north and east to eastern Canada and south into Mexico. This darker Montezuma's Grasshopper (*S. montezuma*) is restricted to the southwest and Mexico, and a third species of *Syrbula* (*S. festiva*, not shown) occurs in Mexico.

# Obscure Birdwing Grasshopper

This grasshopper on a South Carolina tree is an Obscure Birdwing Grasshopper—*Schistocerca obscura*, one of 10 North American species of bird grasshoppers (*Schistocerca* spp., family Acrididae) called birdwings because of their large size and powerful flight. Most *Schistocerca* species are solitary, but one Old World species, *Schistocerca gregaria*, is called the Desert Locust because it responds to crowded conditions by developing a gregarious long-winged form or migratory phase. Migratory-phase locusts can form swarms covering hundreds of square miles, wiping out crops and devastating livelihood across large areas.

# Monkey Grasshopper



Monkey hoppers such as this brightly colored Costa Rican species have an outsized head that seems to stick up above the body, and they usually hold their disproportionately long hind legs out at right angles to the body. Monkey hoppers make up a family of about 1,000 almost entirely tropical species in the family Eumastacidae.

# Jumping Stick

Jumping sticks (family Proscopiidae) form an exclusively neotropical family of wingless stick-like grasshoppers, with about 130 species found in a variety of habitats in South America. The male of this pair is typical of the family, being much smaller than the female. Jumping sticks usually have incredibly strange heads (see inset), with bulbous eyes, tiny antennae and bulging "jowls" that have led some American entomologists to nickname them "Nixon grasshoppers."

# Horse Lubber

The family Romaleidae is a mostly neotropical group of short-horned grasshoppers often called lubber grasshoppers. Lubbers are large, foul-tasting hoppers that can hiss and emit a conspicuous stinky foam from the sides of the thorax (the spiracles) when threatened. This is a nymphal Horse Lubber (*Taeniopoda eques*), a species found from the American southwest through to Central America.

# Green Lubber Grasshopper

The short-horned grasshopper family Romaleidae includes about 200 species, most of which occur in South and Central America, like this bright green *Chromacris* from Costa Rica. Neotropical members of this family are often very large, long-winged insects, in contrast to the single member of the family found in eastern North America, a short-winged flightless species called the Eastern Lubber.

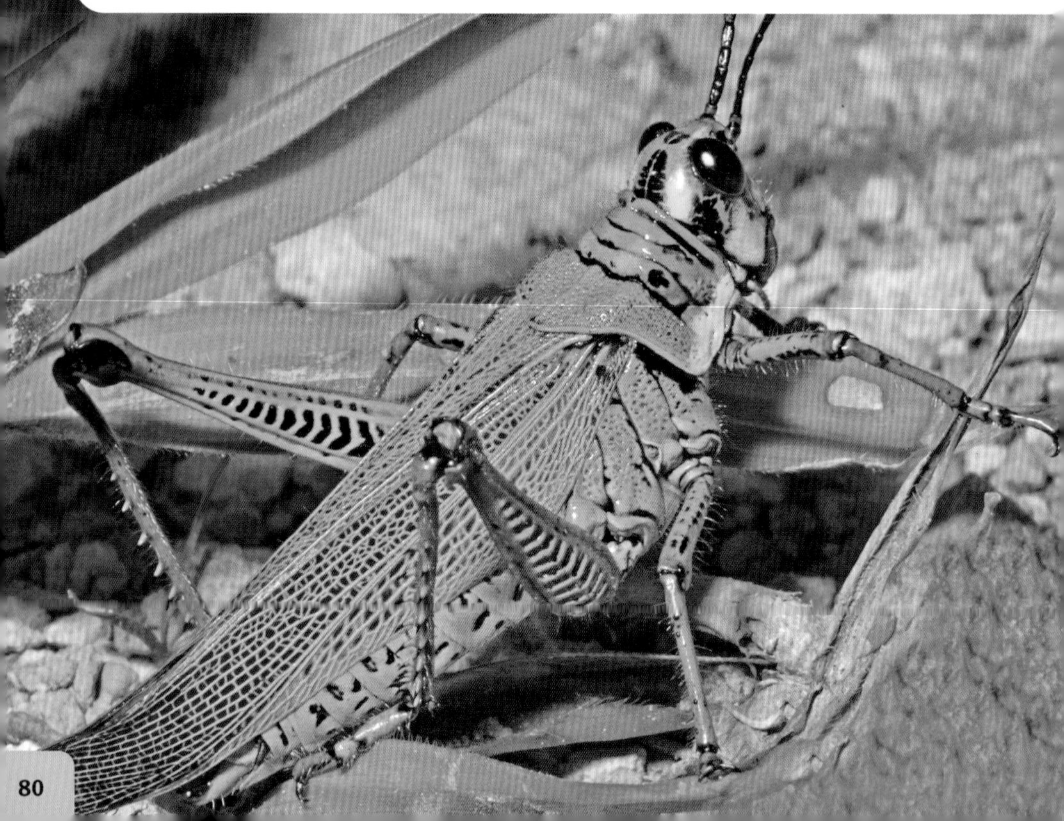

# Plains Lubber Grasshopper

One of the few members of the mostly neotropical family Romaleidae to reach North America, the Plains Lubber Grasshopper (*Brachystola magna*) ranges from Mexico north into the American midwest. These fat flightless hoppers are among the heaviest insects found in North America. Plains Lubber Grasshoppers occur in open areas with sparse vegetation, where they feed on a variety of plants and even the occasional insect.

# Robust Toad Lubber

Grasshoppers found on open gravelly ground or cobble are often well camouflaged in their natural habitat; this Robust Toad Lubber (*Phrynotettix robustus*, family Romaleidae) is inconspicuous against the open ground of a roadside in the Arizona desert. This bulky (fat and often more than 2 inches/5 cm long) hopper ranges from Mexico north to New Mexico, Arizona and Texas.

# Andean Grasshopper



The apparently barren ground high in the Chilean Andes supports a variety of specialized insects, of which the largest are the bulky, slow-moving grasshoppers in the exclusively South American family Ommexechidae. The male of this pair of *Aucacris eumera* has a red mite on the side of his thorax.

# Spear-headed Grasshopper

The spear-headed grasshoppers in the family Pyrgomorphidae form a widespread, mostly tropical group sometimes called gaudy grasshoppers—several species are inedible and advertise their bad taste with bright colors, although this common Amazonian species (*Omura congrua*) has a relatively muted appearance. Pyrgomorphidae are often seen in couples because males guard their mates through long copulations, spending as many as 17 days mounted on a female.

# Pygmy Grasshopper

Pygmy grasshoppers (Tetrigidae), such as this attractively camouflaged Costa Rican *Chiriquia serrata*, are smaller than most grasshoppers, and are often overlooked because of their size and their habit of staying close to the damp ground on which they live as algal grazers. They have a shield made from the pronotum (the top of the first segment behind the head) that extends the length of the body.

# Pygmy Mole Cricket

Pygmy mole crickets and mud crickets (superfamily Tridactyloidea, more closely related to grasshoppers than to crickets) are small (usually less than 0.4 inch/1 cm long) insects usually found along the edges of streams or in other wet areas. Although diverse and common in tropical areas, they remain very poorly known, perhaps because of their small size, nocturnal habits and elusive behavior. These neotropical Ripipterygidae, like the similar but more widely distributed Tridactylidae, can fly, jump, swim and sometimes even burrow.

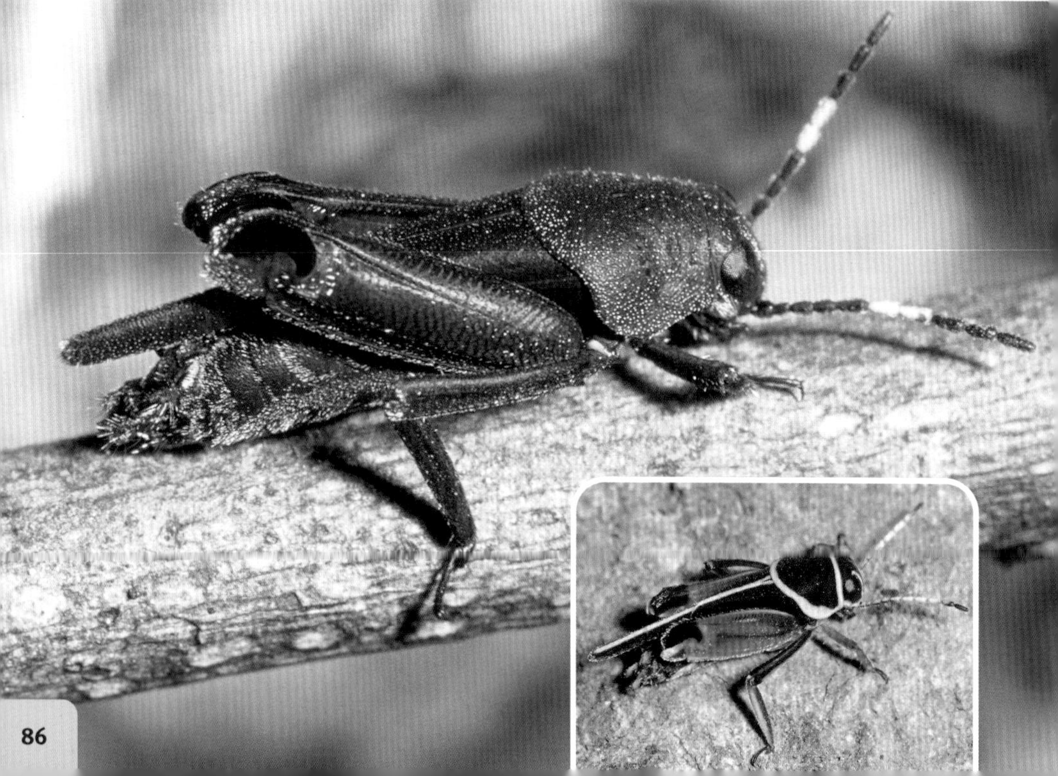

# Water Strider

This small water strider (*Trepobates* sp.) has just molted from the nymphal to the adult stage, although the adult and nymph of this wingless bug are very similar. The newly emerged adult, with its hind legs still in the shed nymphal skin (exuviae), is pale and soft (teneral) but will harden into a blue-black water-skating predator.

# Water Strider

Like all true bugs (Hemiptera, suborder Heteroptera) associated with shorelines or the water surface, water striders (family Gerridae) are predators that use their beaks to pierce the bodies of other insects. The short, stout beak on this eastern North American *Trepobates* is conspicuously swung beneath its head, ready to stab other insects on or just under the surface of the water.

# Water Strider



Water striders (Family Gerridae) often occur as both wingless and fully winged adults, with fully winged individuals, like these *Tachygerris opacus*, more common in ephemeral habitats. This pair was photographed on a puddle in the middle of a rainforest trail in Bolivia, far from the nearest permanent water.

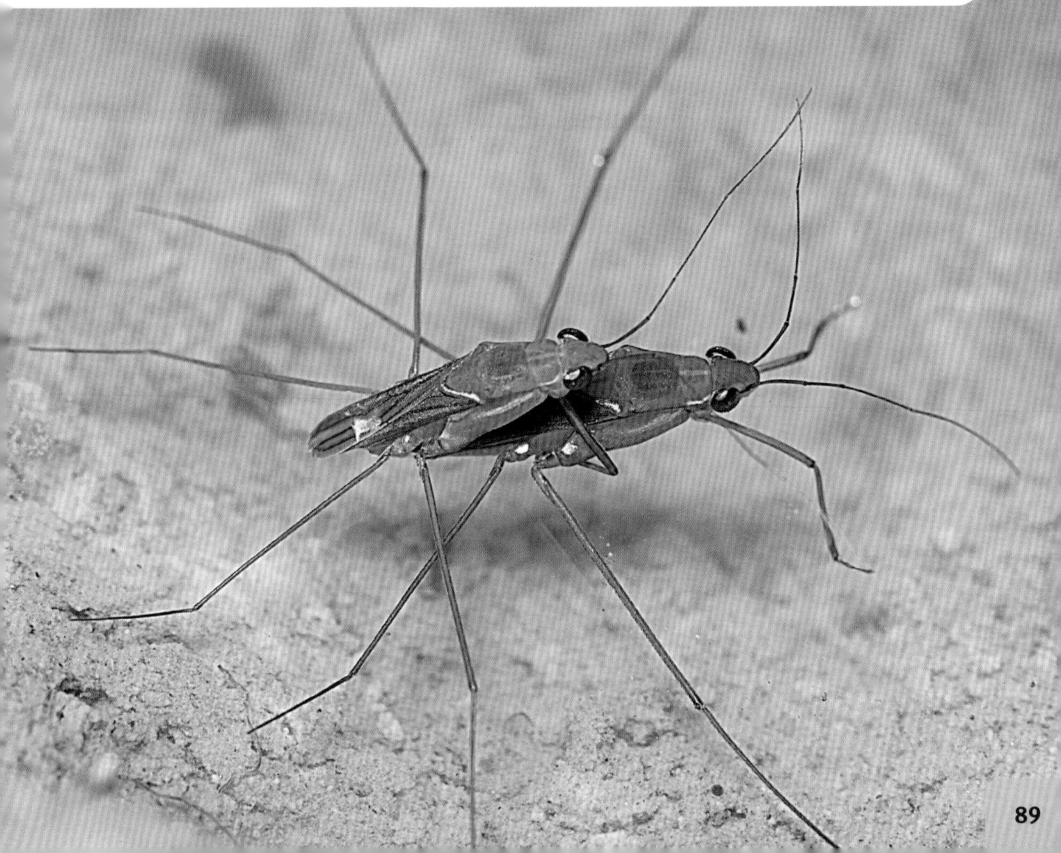

# Water Strider

Many insect species are sexually dimorphic, but few exhibit the spectacular differences between males and females seen in the water strider genus *Rheumatobates* (family Gerridae). Males of this widespread genus, found on surfaces of ponds and lakes, have strikingly modified legs and antennae. This pair of *R. rileyi* is from Canada.

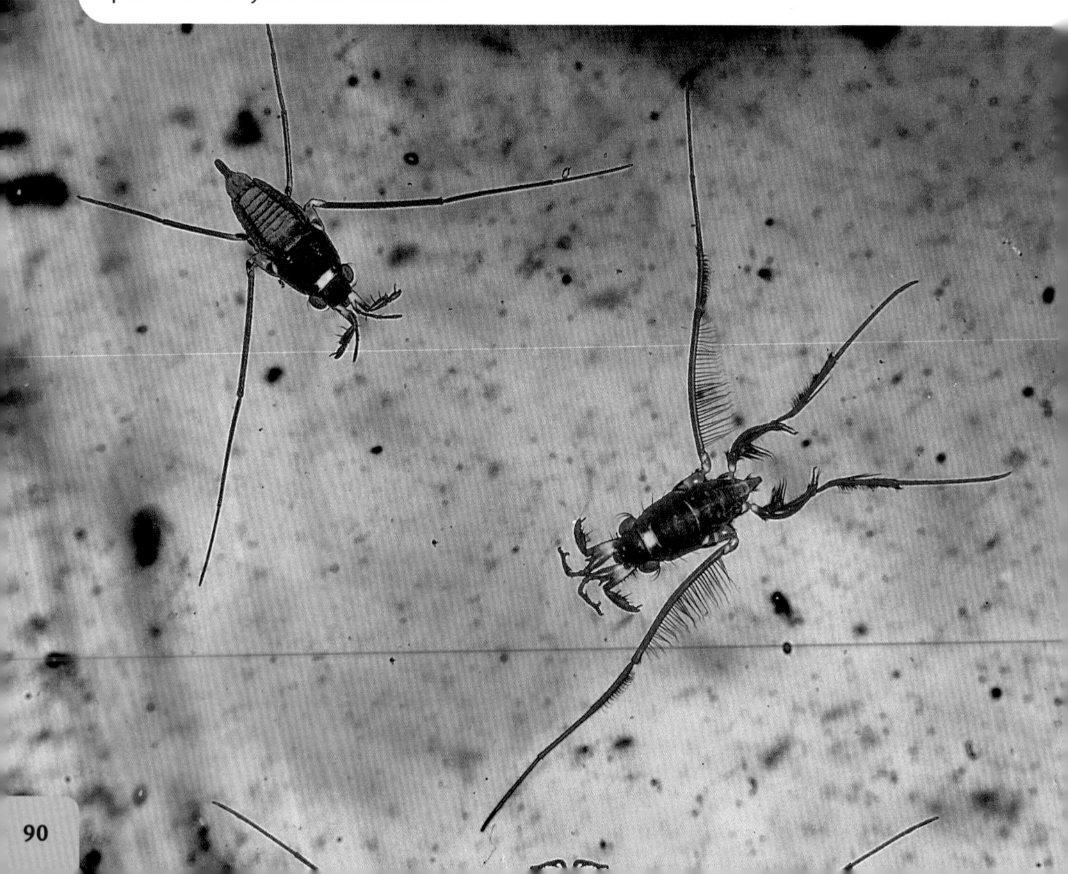

# Water Strider

These water strider nymphs (*Gerris* sp., family Gerridae) are feeding on a dead backswimmer (*Notonecta* sp., family Notonectidae) in an algae-choked pond. Water striders normally feed by using their piercing beaks to spear both living and dead insects; backswimmers are also true bugs and use their piercing beaks to impale living prey ranging from mosquito larvae to small fish.

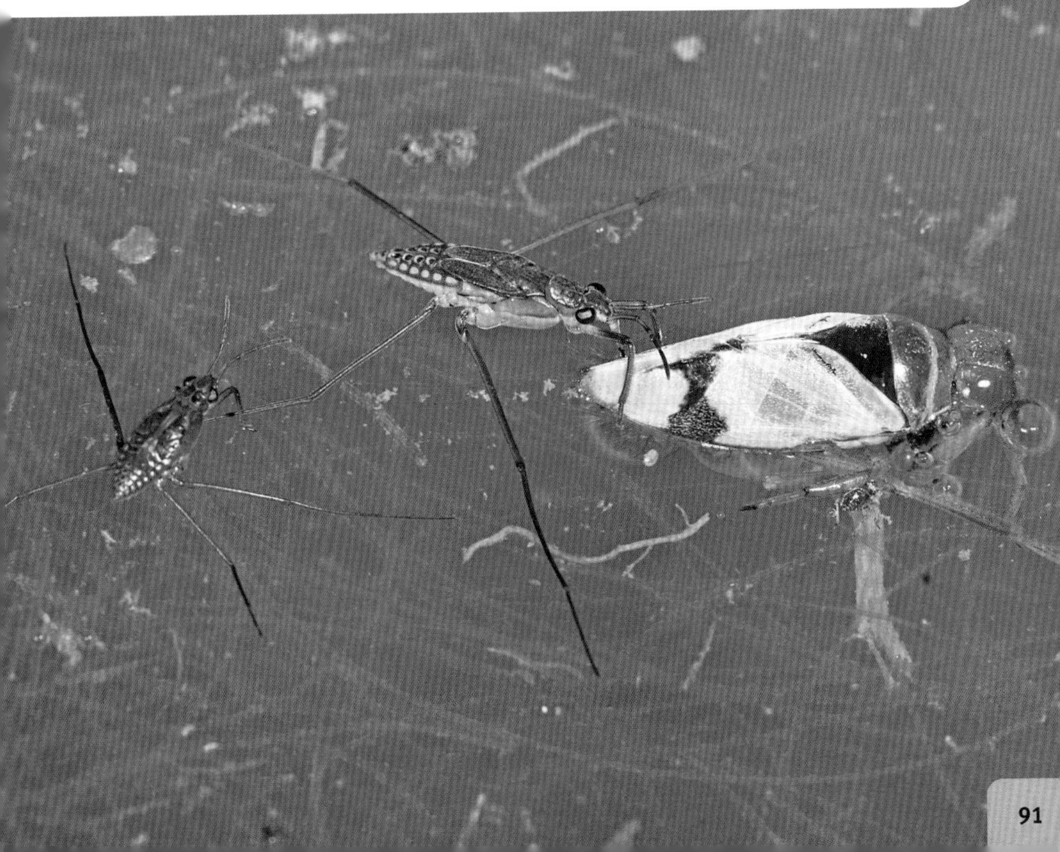

# Giant Water Bug

Giant water bugs in the genus *Lethocerus* (family Belostomatidae) are sometimes called giant electric-light bugs because the big adult bugs often fly into porch lights during flights from pond to pond, presumably mistaking them for moonlight reflecting from an inviting pond. This nymph of *Lethocerus americanus*, a common North American species, is feeding on a fish, demonstrating the stout forelegs and powerful piercing mouthparts that justify the other common name for these big bugs—toe biters.

# Creeping Water Bug

Creeping water bugs (family Naucoridae), such as this *Pelocoris* from a slow North Carolina river, are piercing-sucking predators equipped to impale other insects or small fish. They have a more ready and painful bite than other aquatic bugs, and should be handled with care.

# Water Boatman

Water boatmen (family Corixidae) are among the most abundant aquatic insects. They often occur by the thousands in ponds and quiet river backwaters, where they use thread-like beaks to feed on algae and small arthropods. This red *Hesperocorixa brimleyi* from South Carolina is unusually bright; most water boatmen the world over have more subtle pigmentation, like the smaller *Sigara* species (inset). The forelegs of water boatmen are short and broad, more like little scoops than normal legs.

# Sycamore Lace Bug

Lace bugs (family Tingidae) are delicate, distinctively sculptured bugs, many of which feed on only a single kind of plant (often a tree). This species, the Sycamore Lace Bug (*Corythuca ciliata*), occurs only on sycamore trees and is the only lace bug found on sycamore trees. Sycamore Lace Bugs are native to eastern North America but were accidentally introduced to Europe in the 1960s, where they are now serious pests of the sycamores widely planted as shade trees in many countries. The lace bugs shown here were among hundreds clustered under loose bark during the winter months, but during the summer Sycamore Lace Bugs feed on the lower surfaces of leaves.

# Largid Bug

Adults of the brightly colored bug *Stenomacra marginella* (family Largidae) are usually seen in ones and twos as they puncture leaves or fruit with their needle-like beaks. Young stages, on the other hand, often occur in great masses of hundreds of nymphs. This adult was photographed in Costa Rica, but the species ranges from Central America to the southern United States.

# Largid Bug

*Arhaphe cicindeloides*, probably North America's most distinctive largid bug (family Largidae), is often glimpsed rapidly running along the ground like an ant or a velvet ant. Despite the species name, which seems to suggest similarity to a tiger beetle, this pretty bug is probably a mimic of the well-armed female velvet ant (velvet ants are stinging wasps with wingless females). This species, one of three *Arhaphe* in the southern United States, occurs in the southwest.

# Largid Bug

This red-rimmed *Largus cinctus* (family Largidae) is sucking sap from a cactus in the Arizona desert. Cacti and other spiny desert plants such as yucca and agave seem to be hospitable places for a number of bugs, especially Largidae and the closely related family Coreidae.

# Cactus Bug

Two American members of the family Coreidae (leaf-footed bugs) are known as cactus bugs, and occur on *Opuntia* cacti. These images show a spiny-legged adult *Narnia femorata* on a cactus (inset) and an adult *Chelinidea vittiger* on an agave. Both species lay eggs on cactus spines; the latter species has been exported to Australia as a possible ally in the fight against introduced *Opuntia* cacti, a serious incursion in that country's rangeland.

# Leaf-footed Bug

Coreids (family Coreidae) use their beaks to suck sap from plants, and this *Leptoscelis pallida* has pierced an unopened *Heliconia* flower in Bolivia. *Leptoscelis pallida* is a common leaf-footed bug on *Heliconia* (false bird-of-paradise) plants in Amazonia.

# Leaf-footed Bug

Bugs in the family Coreidae are called leaf-footed bugs because parts of the hind leg of many species are swollen or flattened. *Leptoglossus phyllopus* is a common eastern North American species with leaf-like tibiae; these were among many on a broad sedge leaf.

# Leaf-footed Bug

Leaf-footed bugs (family Coreidae) and the closely related family Alydidae (broad-headed bugs) are harmless sap-sucking bugs that often conceal their lack of defensive weapons with a remarkable similarity to stinging wasps found in the same places. These two Bolivian bugs fooled me in flight, and even look much like ichneumonid wasps when resting on foliage.

# Rice Bug

Rice bugs (*Stenocoris* sp., family Alydidae) are slender bugs found on rice and a variety of wild grasses. This one was photographed in the southeastern United States, but related rice bugs are found around the world, often damaging cultivated rice.

# Milkweed Bug

The bright colors of these orange and black Milkweed Bugs (*Oncopeltus fasciatus*, family Lygaeidae) advertise their toxicity, warning potential predators to steer clear. Like Monarch butterflies and several other insects that feed on milkweed, these bugs are able not only to feed on the relatively toxic plant but also to take in its bitter and poisonous protective compounds and use them for their own defense.

# Boxelder Bug

Boxelder Bugs (*Boisea trivittata*) feed on the seeds of boxelder or Manitoba maple across North America, and often occur in impressively dense mixed aggregations of nymphs and adults. Adults move into sheltered places to spend the winter, often becoming a nuisance when they collect in a garage or front porch. These harmless insects belong to a family of bugs called the scentless plant bugs (family Rhopalidae).

# Seed Bug

The long, sword-like beaks slung under the heads of these bugs look deadly, but they are used only for piercing seeds. Like most members of this family (Rhyparochromidae), the species shown here—a black *Mydocha serripes* from Canada and a close relative from Costa Rica—are ground-dwelling seed predators that feed mostly on fallen mature seeds.

# Four-lined Plant Bug

Four-lined plant bugs, *Poecilocapsus lineatus* (family Miridae), use their beaks to poke into the leaves of a wide variety of garden plants, whipping up the leaf tissue into a chlorophyll-rich slurry they can suck up through straw-like mouthparts. These minor pests (it takes a lot of them to seriously injure a plant) are bright red when they hatch from their eggs in spring, but later turn into adults with attractive yellowish green and black stripes.

# Plant Bug

The bright colors of some plant bugs, such as this *Lopidea* from Arizona, send a warning to potential predators, and for at least some *Lopidea* species it is an honest warning about chemical defenses. Birds display an aversion to feeding on some *Lopidea* species, demonstrating the effectiveness of several compounds that exude from glands on the bug's thorax.

# Stink Bug



Stink bugs, so called because of their well-developed scent glands, or repugnatorial glands, are often conspicuous shield-shaped bugs. Many are brightly colored, presumably to warn potential predators that they taste awful. These colorful stink bugs (family Pentatomidae) from Costa Rica are a boldly spotted *Brachystethus rubromaculatus* (inset) and a pair of blue-green *Edessa*.

# Stink Bug

Stink bugs are tremendously diverse in the tropics, with over a thousand species in South America alone. This Bolivian bug belongs to the genus *Edessa*; this abundant and common group, one of the largest genera in the family, contains many unnamed species.

# Stink Bug

Stink bugs (family Pentatomidae) are mostly plant-sucking insects, but some are predators that use their beaks to pierce and suck other insects. This caterpillar-sucking nymph of *Apateticus cynicus* is obviously in the latter group; the green bug (*Thyanta* sp., inset) on goldenrod is a plant-feeding species. These are both common North American stink bugs.

# Four-humped Stink Bug

Brochymenas, also known as Rough Stink Bugs or Tree Stink Bugs, are superbly camouflaged on their usual tree-branch or tree-trunk haunts. These are Four-humped Stink Bugs, *Brochymena quadripustulata*. Brochymenas feed mostly on caterpillars.

# Stink Bug

Bugs often lay clusters of large, barrel-shaped eggs that attract a variety of potential parasitoids and predators, which explains why some bugs, such as this Costa Rican stink bug, stay with their eggs and guard them from enemies. Nymphs of a few species stay under their mother's protection for some time after hatching. The nymphs shown here emerging from eggs (inset) belong to a North American stink bug species (family Pentatomidae) that does not exhibit parental care.

# Shield-backed Bug

Shield-backed bugs (family Scutelleridae) resemble the closely related stink bugs, but the entire back part of the body is covered by a dome-like shield derived from the scutellum (normally triangular plate on top of the bug that projects back between the wings). Tropical shield bugs, like this one from Australia, are often outrageously colorful, presumably to advertise their potent stink glands.

# Dinidorid Bug

This Costa Rican bug looks much like a stink bug, but it belongs to a related small family of plant-feeding bugs, the Dinidoridae. Several families of broad-bodied odorous bugs, often with a similar broad-shouldered or shield-shaped appearance, are grouped together as the superfamily Pentatomoidea.

# Canopid Bug

*Canopus* species (family Canopidae) feed on the sporophores of fungi. Both adult and immature bugs occur on fungi, and adults such as this one, photographed in Bolivia, are often seen in flight or on foliage. Canopidae is a small neotropical family related to shield bugs and stink bugs.

# Kissing Bug



This is a "kissing bug" (*Panstrongylus* sp., subfamily Triatominae, family Reduviidae) from Central America, but stay out from under the mistletoe with it unless you want to end up with Chagas' disease. Chagas' disease is also called American trypanosomiasis because the causative organism is a trypanosome (a microscopic organism) transmitted through the feces of these bloodsucking bugs in Central and South America.

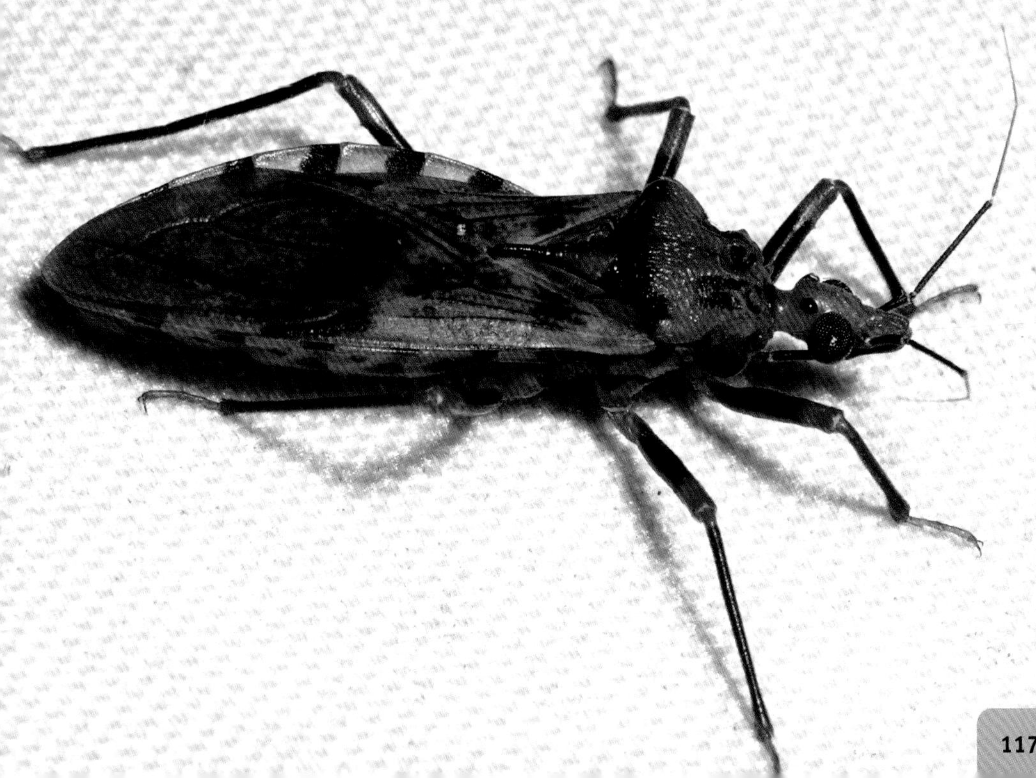

# Assassin Bug

This assassin bug, a brightly colored *Castolus tricolor* from Costa Rica, is a predator that impales other insects with its stout beak, injecting enzymes that kill and dissolve its prey so the victim's contents can be imbibed as though through a straw. Assassin bugs can inflict painful bites if handled carelessly.

# Assassin Bug

This South American assassin bug (family Reduviidae) belongs to the widespread genus *Zelus*, which also includes species common in United States and Canada. This species, however, bears a remarkable similarity to some wasps and micropezid flies (*Scipopus* spp.) seen at the same place and time in a Bolivian rainforest. It likely gains some protection from predators by being part of a mimicry complex.

# Assassin Bug

This short-winged assassin bug (family Reduviidae, subfamily Ectrichodiinae) was found under the trunk of a fallen tree in the Bolivian rainforest, where it presumably impales small arthropods with its stout beak. Bug beaks are made up of four narrow blades (mandibles and maxillae) sitting in a sheath made from the lower lip (labium). The maxillae come together to create a two-channeled straw, with one channel for injection and one for ingestion.

# Damsel Bug



Bugs in the small family Nabidae are called damsel bugs, but, as demonstrated by this North American *Hoplistoscelis sordidus* eating a barklouse, they are more dragon-like than damsel-like in their interactions with other insects. Some are such voracious predators that they are welcomed as natural control agents of insect pests in orchards and elsewhere.

# Gnat Bug

Gnat bugs or unique-headed bugs (family Enicocephalidae) are common insects of neotropical cloud forests. Normally they remain hidden under stones and logs but are occasionally seen on foliage or in swarms similar to those formed by midges (or gnats). The head is indeed unique, looking more like that of a balloon animal than a bug and ending in a prominent beak that functions to impale small prey. These tiny, inconspicuous insects are the most primitive true bugs (Heteroptera) and are represented in the fossil record back to 125 million years ago.

# Treehopper

Treehoppers seem to be well-protected throughout their lives. Eggs, like this batch of *Entylia carinata* eggs, are often guarded by the adult female (see inset), and nymphs (young hoppers between the egg stage and the adult stage) are often tended in groups by ants that guard them in exchange for the sugary waste products (honeydew) pooped out by the treehopper nymphs. The *Myrmica* ant shown here is tending newly hatched *Entylia* nymphs right on the egg mass. Adults are protected by a single piece of armor (the pronotum) that extends back from just behind the head, often over the entire body. *Entylia carinata* is one of the most common treehoppers in North America.

# Treehopper

Females of many treehoppers (family Membracidae) such as these two *Pubililia concava* take care of their eggs and young nymphs, protecting them from parasitic wasps and other parasitoids and predators. Females of some species release an attractant chemical as they lay eggs, luring other females to lay eggs in the same place. This is a common North American species, often abundant on weeds and usually attended by ants.

# Treehopper



Treehoppers (family Membracidae) are often protected from parasitoids by ants in exchange for the sweet honeydew egested by the sap-sucking hoppers. These images from Bolivia show some treehoppers in the genus *Horolia* tended by *Dolichoderus* ants.

# Treehopper

Treehoppers (family Membracidae) such as this shiny black and yellow *Darnis partita* from Costa Rica all have a greatly enlarged pronotum. The pronotum is the top (notum) of the first segment of the thorax (prothorax), and in this case it makes a shining yellow and black shield extending over much of the body.

# Treehopper



Treehoppers in the genus *Heteronotus* (family Membracidae) occur from Mexico to Argentina; this *H. nodosus* was photographed in Bolivia. The elaborate pronotal shield that extends over the top of the body looks enough like an ant to deter ant-shy potential predators.

# Treehopper

The pronotal shields of tropical treehoppers (family Membracidae) are often divided and ornamented to form an intimidating spiked parasol, sometimes with an overall shape that gives the shield a remarkably antlike appearance. This elegant *Bocydium* was one of many along the weedy margin of a Costa Rican cloud-forest road.

# Treehopper

Treehoppers in the genus *Notocera*, such as this *N. spinidorsa* from Bolivia, are small (0.16–0.24 inches/4–6 mm) but spectacularly adorned with horns and other body adornments such as humps and spines, flattened legs and white waxy coverings. *Notocera* species, like many other hoppers, communicate between the sexes by way of vibrations transmitted through plant stems or leaves.

# Treehopper

This Bolivian *Cyphonia trifida* (family Membracidae) has a spectacular black-and-white pronotal shield that would probably be an uncomfortable mouthful for a hungry bird or lizard, and the swellings and spines on the pronotal shield of this Costa Rican *Cyphonia clavata* (inset) make it look like a particularly unpalatable and aggressive ant. Like all treehoppers, *Cyphonia* species suck sap from plants. The biology of this widespread neotropical genus is otherwise poorly known.

# Treehopper



*Membracis* species are often big, colorful treehoppers with a large, flat, keel-like pronotum. Unlike most treehoppers, which communicate by tapping the substrate, *Membracis* males produce sound by buzzing their wings as they approach potential mates. This group of adult *Membracis tectigera* along with a white nymph are from Bolivia, but *Membracis* species are widespread in the neotropics and the Caribbean.

# Treehopper

This female treehopper (*Guayaquila* sp., family Membracidae) is tending an egg mass covered with a waxy, sticky secretion; she will stay with the eggs until the nymphs hatch. Several females frequently occupy the same plant, often along with ants that protect them from predators and parasites in exchange for honeydew egested by the treehoppers. This egg-tending female is from Bolivia and this pair of similar treehoppers clinging to a stem (inset) is from Costa Rica. Related *Guayaquila* species occur throughout the neotropics.

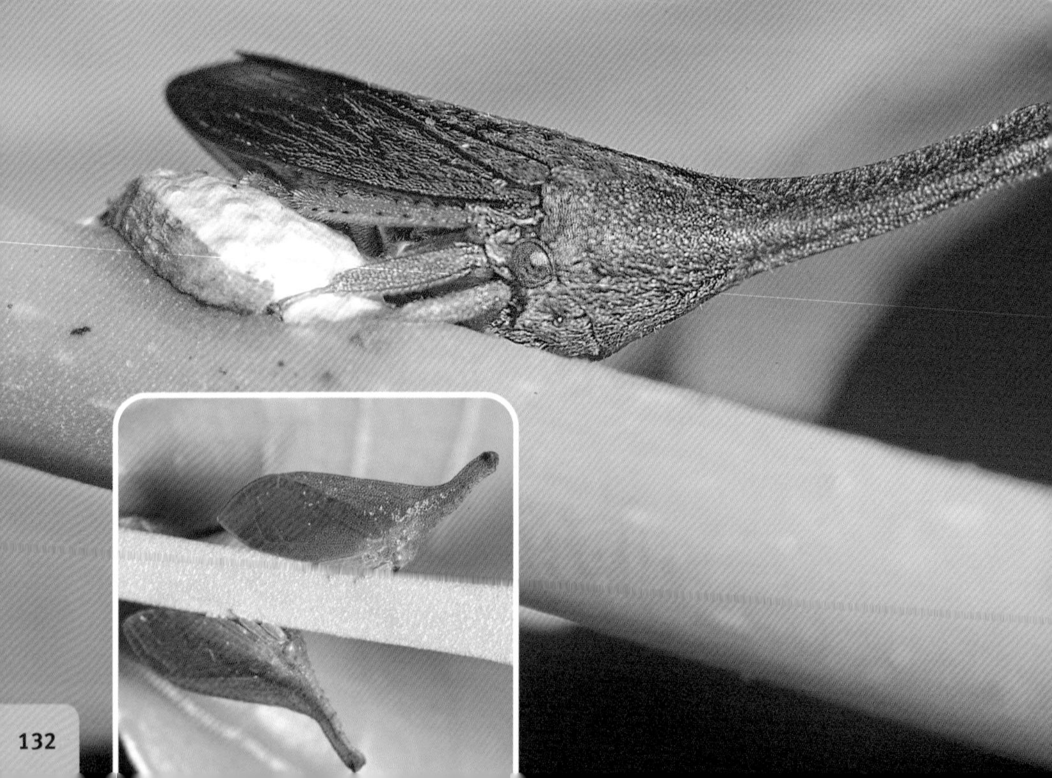

# Treehopper



This Bolivian treehopper (*Hemikyptha* sp., family Membracidae) is a large, well-armed insect that would certainly present a spiky mouthful to most potential vertebrate predators. The intimidatingly spiked shield that covers much of the body is an expanded pronotum, as is typical for the family.

# Buffalo Treehopper

Nymphs of treehoppers, like this common North American Buffalo Treehopper (*Ceresa alta* = *Stictocephala alta*), often look quite unlike the distinctively shield-backed adults. Buffalo Treehopper nymphs (inset) are common in weeds near fruit trees; adults occur in the trees, where they lay eggs in the twigs with their sharp ovipositors.

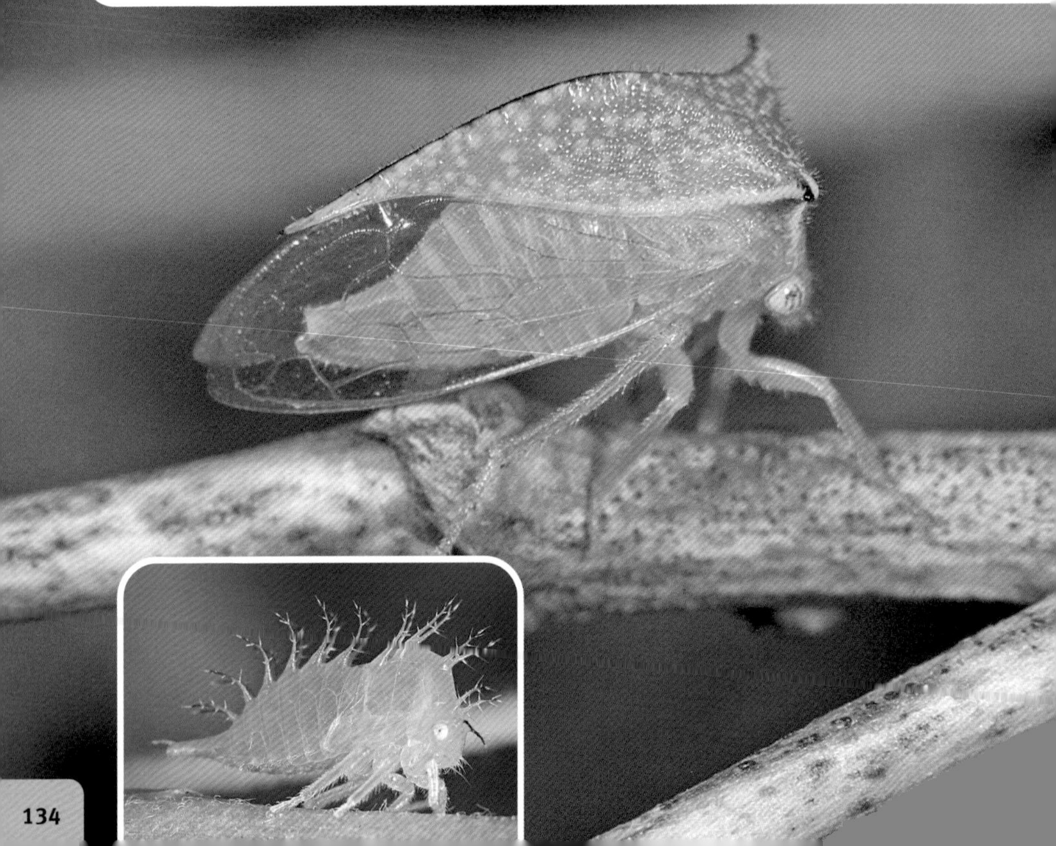

# Treehopper

This beautiful orange, black and white treehopper species, *Phyllotropis fasciata* occurs in South America, Central America and even the Caribbean. The distinctively long and slender treehoppers in the genus *Polyglypta* (inset), found from Mexico to Brazil, often occur in aggregations of several individuals, even laying eggs in communal masses inserted into leaf veins.

# Treehopper

This treehopper (family Membracidae, genus *Amastris*) is hunkered down over an extrafloral nectary on a Bolivan *Inga* leaf, probably sucking sap through the surrounding swollen tissue. Extrafloral nectaries are pots of sugary fluids produced by some plants to attract ants that in turn protect the leaves from being eaten by caterpillars (see also pages 360, 498).

# Treehopper



This Costa Rican treehopper (*Aetalion*) is tending a batch of eggs while recently hatched nymphs cluster not far off. The bright orange blob near the tip of her abdomen is a mite. Treehoppers in the genus *Aetalion* are sometimes grouped with other treehoppers in the family Membracidae but are more often treated as part of a separate family, Aetalionidae.

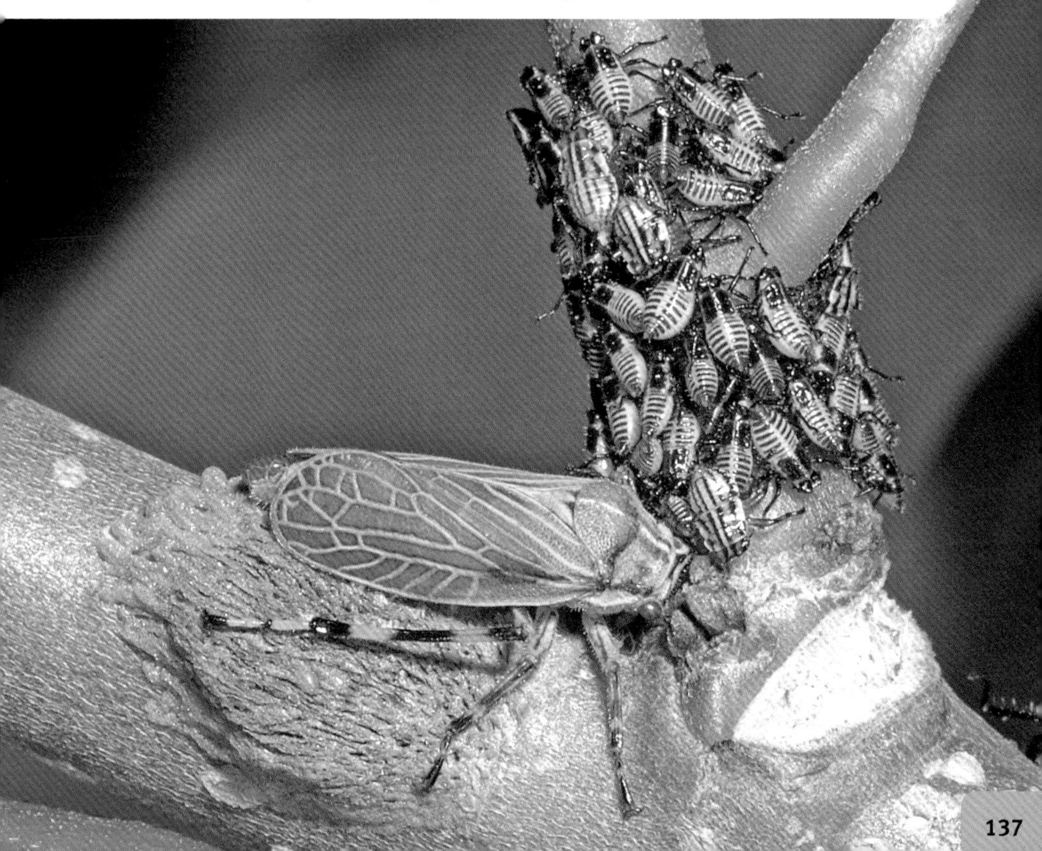

# Planthopper

Tropical planthoppers in the family Flatidae, like this one from Costa Rica, are often superficially similar to small moths, although of course they lack scales on the wings and have typical sucking-bug mouthparts.

# Lanternfly



Lanternflies, or peanut bugs, are among the best-known insects of the New World tropics because of their size (3 inches/7.6 cm) and spectacular peanut-shaped "nose," which is threateningly marked like the head of an alligator or lizard—complete with teeth and eyes. Contrary to popular belief, lanternflies do not produce light and they do not bite (no planthopper can bite), but they can put on a good startle display by exposing their eye-like hind wings.

# Planthopper

Planthoppers form a group of related families that are generally inconspicuous in temperate regions but explode into a profusion of color and form in the tropics. This charismatically long-nosed *Odontoptera carrenoi* belongs to the same family (Fulgoridae) as the lanternflies, or peanut bugs. Like most other planthoppers (superfamily Fulgoroidea), it feeds using a straw-like beak to suck sap from plants.

# Planthopper

This large, superbly camouflaged planthopper looks like many South American species in the mostly tropical family Fulgoridae, but it is a western North American species (*Alphina glauca*). Large planthoppers such as this one are uncommon in North America, but a similar species, *Calyptoproctus marmoratus*, occurs in the eastern United States.

# Planthopper

Planthoppers are mostly tropical, but a few fairly exotic-looking forms are temperate, and several species of spectacularly long-nosed *Scolops* (family Dictyopharidae) range north to Canada. They are often common in meadows, such as the *Rudbeckia* meadow in central Ontario where this *S. sulcipes* was photographed.

# Planthopper

This brilliant green *Acanalonia* (family Issidae) looks very similar to the eastern North American *Acanalonia conica*, and this transparent-winged dictyopharid (family Dictyopharidae, inset) looks very much like the North American species *Nersia florens*. Both, however, were photographed in the Bolivian rainforest and both are probably undescribed species. Despite a constant stream of published discoveries by planthopper specialists such as Dr. Lois O'Brien, many neotropical planthoppers remain unknown to science.

# Planthopper

Nymphs of many planthoppers (superfamily Fulgoroidea) produce wax from abdominal glands, and colorful nymphs trailing tails of waxy filaments are a regular sight in tropical forests. This nymph (family Issidae) was one of many seen along a cloud forest trail in Costa Rica.

# Planthopper



This mobile foamy mass inching its way along a plant stem in the Bolivian rainforest is a planthopper nymph sucking sap from under the protection of a white wax shelter. Nymphs of many planthoppers (superfamily Fulgoroidea) produce wax from abdominal glands, but few produce such elaborate and all-encompassing waxy mobile homes.

# Planthopper

Planthoppers, such as this brown and pink *Anotia* (family Derbidae, inset) from Cuba and this unidentified waxy Costa Rican species, are distinct from leafhoppers and treehoppers in having a strong carina (ridge) in front of each eye. *Anotia* and some similar attractive derbids also occur in North America, but most other temperate planthoppers are relatively inconspicuous.

# Planthopper

Some planthoppers, such as these Bolivian derbids (family Derbidae, tribe Mysidini), form mating aggregations called leks, away from their host plants. These derbids were using the underside of a broad leaf near the edge of a forest as a sort of fulgoroid pickup bar; the same surface was also being used as a lek site by some small flies (family Clusiidae).

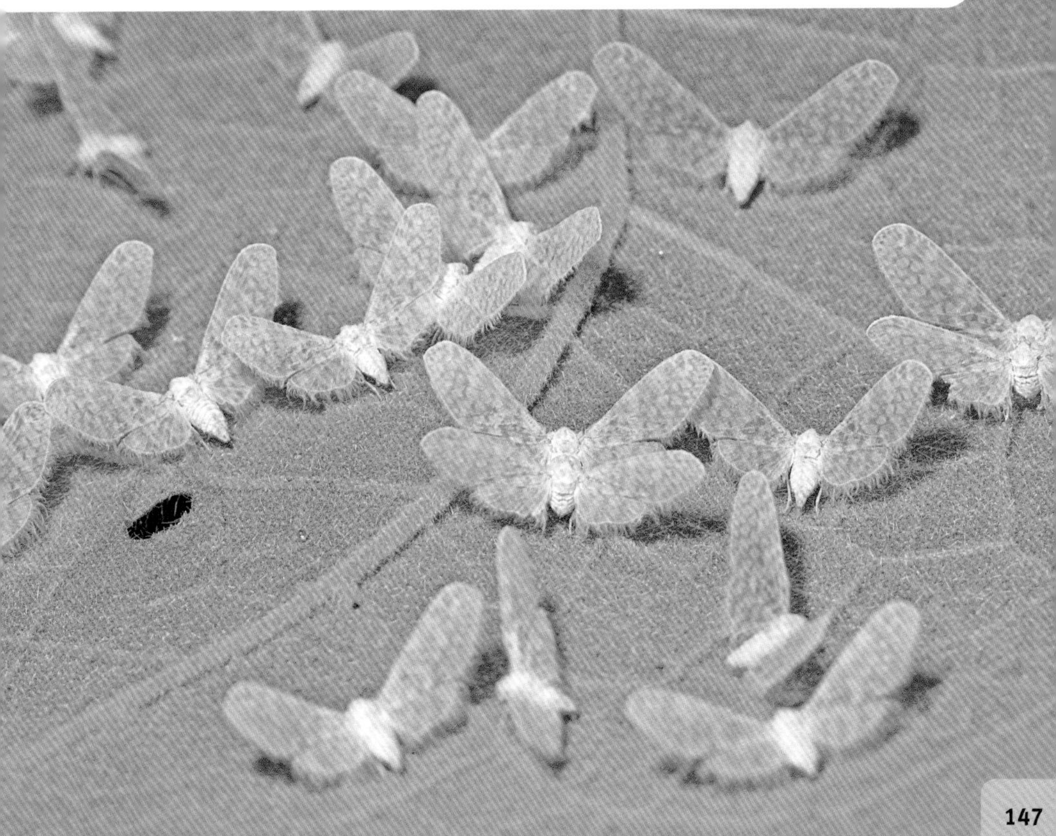

# Planthopper

Some planthoppers such as this Bolivian mysidine derbid (family Derbidae) resemble small moths in posture and color. Unlike moths, they lack wing scales and of course differ from moths in having a beak, which is used to pierce plants and suck sap.

# Planthopper



This Costa Rican planthopper (*Nogodina* sp.) belongs to the tropical family Nogodinidae, a small and relatively little-known family found throughout South and Central America.

# Planthopper

Adult planthoppers in the family Cixiidae, such as this bluish *Mnemosyne* from Peru and this unidentified orange and brown Costa Rican hopper, are often conspicuous as adults, but their nymphs usually live concealed beneath the ground, where they feed on roots.

# Planthopper

This achilid planthopper (*Plectoderes* sp., family Achilidae) from Bolivia is boldly and conspicuously colored, but orange and black are common warning colors, sported by fireflies, net-winged beetles and other chemically protected insects. The colors displayed by this *Plectoderes* might deter predators even if it is not itself an unpalatable species.

# Planthopper

Many planthoppers, such as this *Megamelanus terminalis* (family Delphacidae) from the eastern United States, are brachypterous, or short-winged. Since they usually remain concealed and close to the ground among thatch or other plant material, these pretty little hoppers are rarely seen.

# Two-lined Spittlebug



Spittlebugs, or froghoppers (family Cercopidae), such as this Two-lined Spittlebug (*Prosapia bicinctus*) use their syringe-like beaks to imbibe xylem from plant stems. Spittlebug nymphs remain feeding head-down in one spot while pumping a mixture of sticky secretions, air and digested sap out their rotating tails. The resulting whipped-up froth flows over the nymph to form a spittle-like bubble shelter (inset).

# Cicada

Cicadas are bigger, noisier and more familiar than the closely related spittlebugs and leafhoppers. Nymphs suck xylem sap from tree roots, spending years underground before emerging as short-lived adults that congregate and feed on tree branches while the males sing loudly with their drumskin-like abdominal tymbals. This brown nymph of *Amphipsalta zealandica*, of one of New Zealand's more than 40 cicada species has just emerged from the ground and will soon transform into a winged adult like the one clinging to the same twig.

# Cicada

Cicadas such as this large Costa Rican *Fidicina mannifera* spend long periods as nymphs, often feeding on tree roots for years before emerging as short-lived adults that suck sap from twigs and branches. Some eastern American species spend 17 years in the nymphal stage before emerging almost synchronously in dense, noisy groups of adults, but most species have shorter life cycles.

# Leafhopper

Leafhoppers (family Cicadellidae) are conspicuously diverse almost everywhere, with an especially spectacular exuberance of forms and colors in the tropics. Low, weedy vegetation along the edges of forests or fields can yield thousands of these speedy little sap-sucking bugs. The colorful species shown here include a blue-banded *Macugonalia moesta* and a long-snouted *Ichthyobelus bellicosus* (inset); both are from Bolivia.

# Leafhopper

The bright patterns of this Peruvian *Dilobopterus* (inset) and the conspicuous wing-spreading behavior of this red-spotted *Ladoffa arcuata* from Costa Rica suggest that color plays an important role in leafhopper biology, but these little bugs also communicate using drum-like structures (tymbals) similar to those used by their much louder and larger relatives, the cicadas. There are about 20,000 named leafhopper (Cicadellidae) species, but at least as many remain to be discovered amongst poorly known tropical faunas.

# Leafhopper

Leafhoppers (family Cicadellidae) in the genus *Lissocarta*, like this Bolivian species (probably *L. pereneensis*), look and behave like common wasps found in the same places. The inset photograph is a polistine wasp (family Vespidae) photographed on the same tree at the same time as the leafhopper. This is apparently a striking case of Batesian mimicry, in which a harmless or edible animal mimics a well-defended or inedible one (if the leafhopper had its own defenses, it would be a Muellerian mimic).

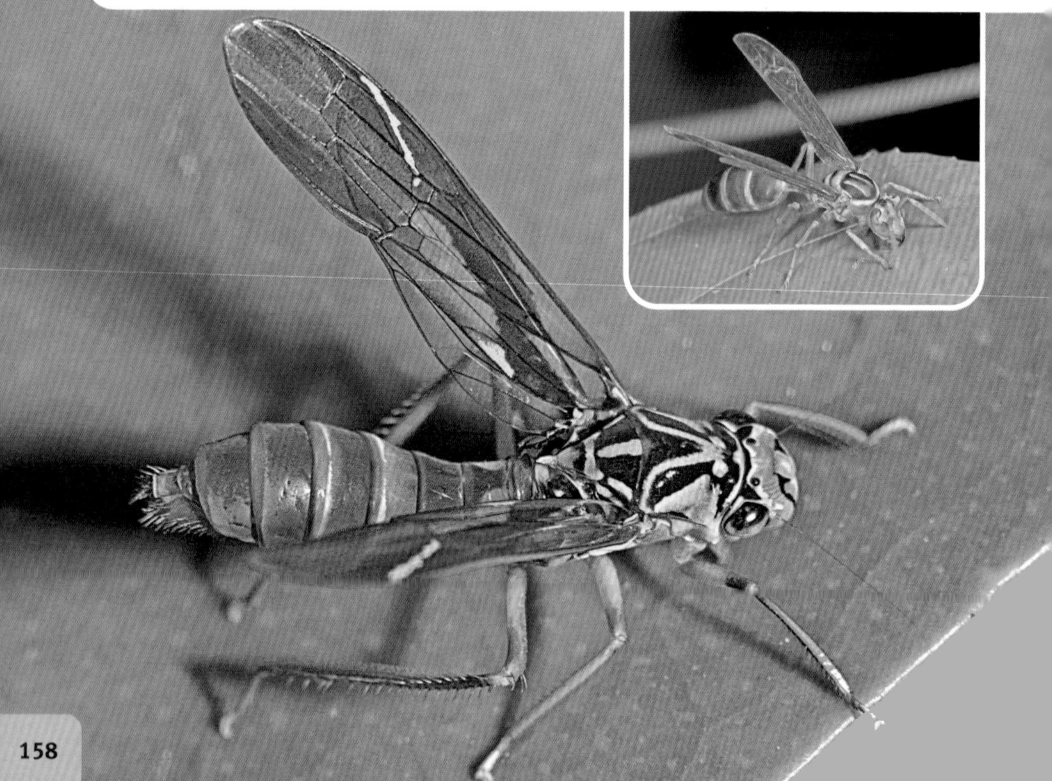

# Leafhopper

A few leafhoppers (family Cicadellidae) routinely "pose" with their wings spread, more like little moths than the typical leafhopper. This orange Bolivian coelidiine (subfamily Coelidiinae) is conspicuous to the point of being garish when it poses with its wings outstretched; it must surely be warning predators that it is unpalatable.

# Leafhopper

This tiny Bolivian leafhopper (*Erythrogonia* sp., family Cicadellidae) was one of many along the edge of a clearing in the rainforest. They were all periodically "displaying" by partly spreading their wings, perhaps to attract mates. Leafhopper mating behaviors are often complex, involving acoustic and visual displays, but are little studied even for common and economically important species.

# Aphid

Aphids feed by sucking phloem sap from plants. Because phloem is sugar-rich but nitrogen-poor, aphid “poop” is a sweet fluid, called honeydew. Aphids are often tended by ants that see the aphids as a valuable source of honeydew, protecting them from parasites and predators.

# Aphid

Aphids, such as these red *Uroleucon* on an Ontario sunflower, usually have two prominent tubes (cornicles, or siphunculi) sticking out from the back of the body. Although those tubes can be used to deliver defensive fluids, aphids are still heavily predated and parasitized. Their main defense is an incredibly rapid rate of reproduction—unfertilized females give birth not to eggs, but to nymphs that will start to feed almost immediately.

# Oleander Aphid



The Oleander Aphid or Milkweed Aphid (*Aphis nerii*) is a common and distinctively colored aphid that feeds on oleander and milkweed, both of which are loaded with toxic steroids called cardiac glycosides. Like other milkweed-feeding insects such as Monarch Butterflies, the aphids take in these toxins for their own defense; they also produce waxy liquids from the tips of their cornicles (the two black tubes sticking out from the aphid's rear). Some natural enemies such as parasitic wasps can get fatally gummed up in the congealing wax, but others, such as the aphid-eating flower fly larva seen here, seem undeterred by the aphid's chemical and physical defenses. This cosmopolitan aphid probably originated in Europe. North American populations are made up entirely of females, which build up populations quickly by giving birth to road-ready nymphs rather than laying eggs.

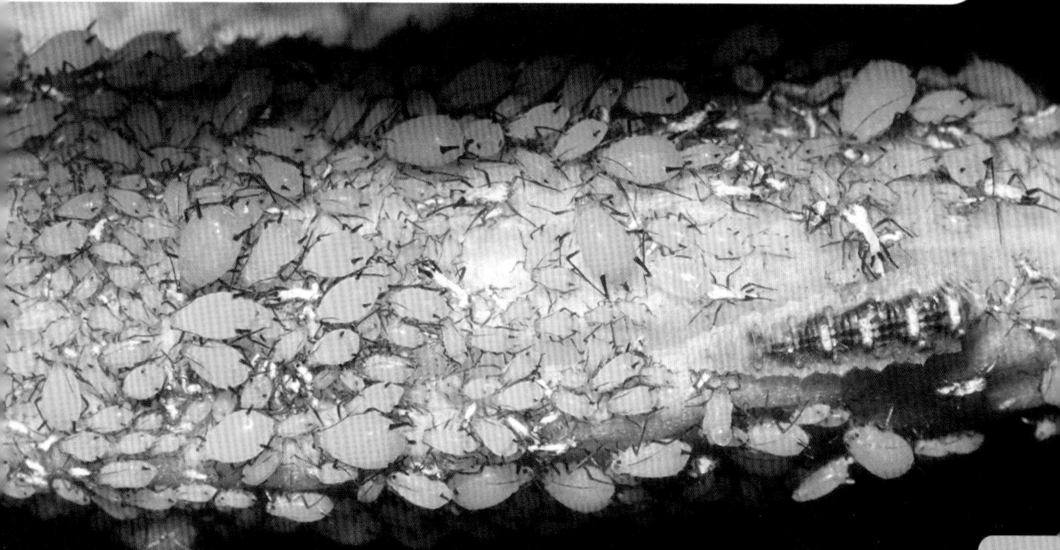

# Cottony Cushion Scale

Scale insects are bugs with piercing-sucking mouthparts, but female scales often have no visible appendages and look more like blobs than bugs. The Cottony Cushion Scale (*Icerya purchasi*, family Margarodidae) is a serious citrus pest accidentally introduced from Australia to California in the late 1800s; it now also occurs in the eastern United States and Caribbean (this photo is from Cuba). The cottony fluted parts are the egg sacs, each containing around a thousand eggs.

# Scale Insect

Waxy filaments are produced by several bug families, including scales, aphids, planthoppers and jumping plant lice. The wax-producing bugs shown here, both from the Ecuadorian rainforest, are scales (superfamily Coccoidea; here tended by ants) and nymphal jumping plant lice (inset).

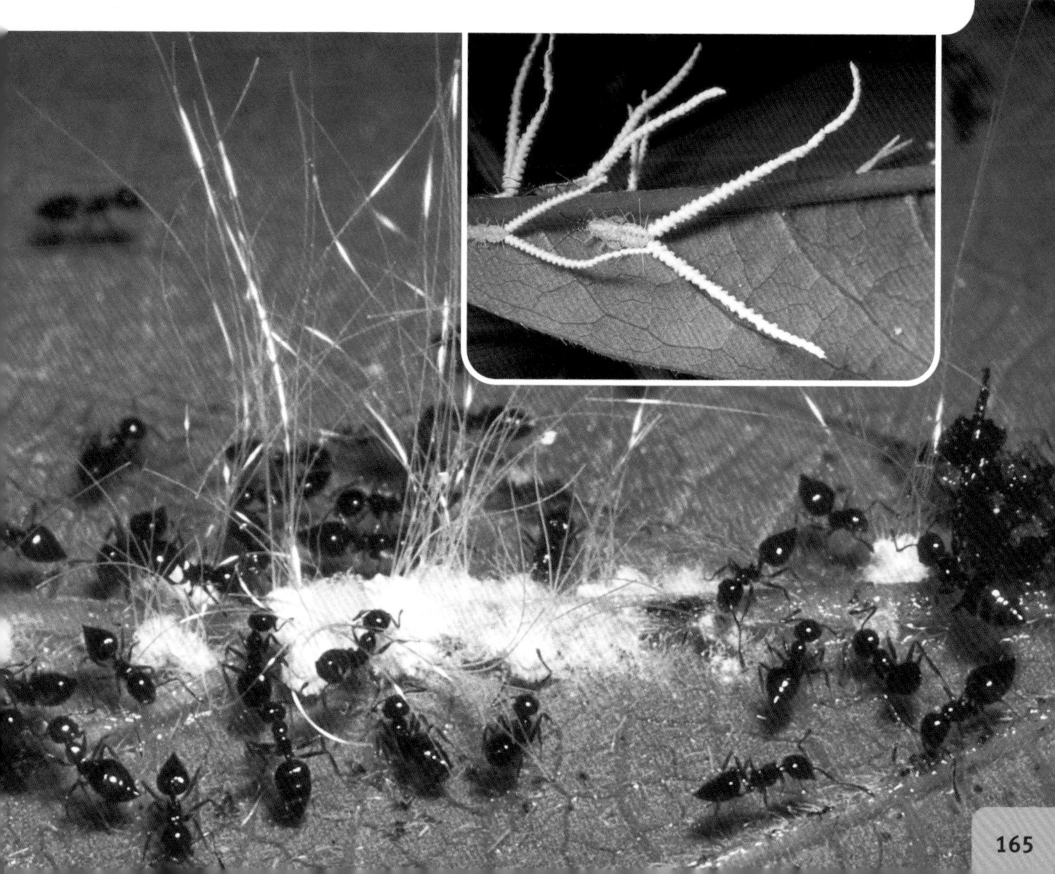

# Barklouse

Barklice (order Psocoptera) are common insects but are often overlooked as they quietly and inconspicuously gnaw away at lichens on tree trunks. As you can see in this photo of a common eastern North American species (*Metylophorus novascotiae*, family Psocidae), barklice have long antennae and a bulging, swollen face.

# Barklouse



Barklice are usually inconspicuous insects, but some of the giant thyrsophorine psocids (subfamily Thyrsophorinae, family Psocidae) of South America, such as this *Poecilopsocus calocoroides* from Bolivia, are unusually large, boldly colored and strikingly humpbacked.

# Thrips

Thrips (order Thysanoptera) are generally inconspicuous insects that are either wingless or have fringed, feather-like wings. Most thrips are tiny, but some tube-tailed thrips (family Phlaeothripidae) are a little bigger; this long, skinny Costa Rican thrips is a whopping 0.2 inch (0.5 cm) in length. This group of somewhat smaller North American *Hoplothrips karnyi* is part of a colony in a hard fungus (inset); males of this species fight each other with their forelegs in defense of egg-laying areas.

# Satyrine Butterfly



The wood nymphs and satyrs (subfamily Satyrinae, family Nymphalidae) form a group of generally grass-feeding, brownish, eyespotted butterflies such as this Cuban *Calisto* (inset). Relatively few satyrs are as brightly colored as this blue Bolivian *Caeruleuptychia*.

# Ithomiine Butterfly

Several different kinds of tropical butterflies have developed a similar clear-winged appearance, but most of the ethereal semitransparent butterflies so often seen (at least momentarily) along cloud-forest pathways belong to the Ithomiinae, a subfamily of Nymphalidae. This is a pair of *Greta morgane* from Costa Rica.

# Viceroy



These mating Viceroys (*Limenitis archippus*) are conspicuous to passing predators, but they are likely to be left alone because their bright red and black colors advertise nasty-tasting defensive chemicals. Unlike the strikingly similar milkweed-feeding Monarchs, which lack the black band across the hind wing, Viceroys are often (but not always) perfectly edible—their colors may constitute false advertising, or Batesian mimicry. Viceroy larvae, which are common on willow and poplar foliage, avoid predation a different way: they look like bird droppings. Viceroys remain common in most of North America but have become rare in some areas.

# Marcella Daggerwing

The daggerwings, a distinctive group of brush-footed butterflies (family Nymphalidae), are most common in Central and South America. This brilliantly colored male Marcella Daggerwing (*Marpesia marcella*) in western Ecuador is uncoiling his straw-like proboscis into what appears to be an extrafloral nectary. Daggerwings are often seen at "puddle parties"—aggregations of butterflies seeking salts around mud puddles or damp soil.

# Hairstreak

The tiny, delicate "gossamer-winged" butterflies in the family Lycaenidae make up about 40 percent of all butterfly species, and comprise an even larger percentage of rare or endangered butterfly species. Many Lycaenidae (those in the subfamily Theclinae) are called hairstreaks because, like this Cuban *Satyrium*, they have tails that look remarkably like heads and antennae. Predators grabbing at these fake heads end up with no more than a bit of wing and a mouthful of scales.

# Metalmark

Butterflies in the family Riodinidae, such as these *Charis gynaea* from Costa Rica, are called metalmarks because their wings are often marked with small metallic-looking spots. Metalmark caterpillars, like larvae of the very closely related Lycaenidae, often have a close relationship with ants, which they feed from special glands in exchange for protection from predators and parasitoids.

# Metalmark

This Bolivian metalmark (family Riodinidae) belongs to the genus *Sarota*, a taxonomically difficult neotropical genus of about 20 species. According to metalmark expert Dr. Philip DeVries, *Sarota* caterpillars are found in wet forests, where at least some species eat leafy mosses and liverworts growing on the upper surfaces of old leaves.

# Metalmark

Although it is represented by only a few species in North America, the metalmark family (Riodinidae) includes a fantastic diversity of butterflies throughout the neotropics. This green-bodied *Caria* was photographed in the Bolivian rainforest.

# Skipper



Skippers (superfamily Hesperoidea), such as this one from Bolivia, are day-flying Lepidoptera closely related to the butterflies (superfamily Papillionoidea). Like many butterflies and moths, skippers are attracted to flowers, from which they sip nectar using a long, coiled proboscis.

# Puriri Moth

This Puriri Moth (*Aenetus virescens*) from New Zealand's North Island belongs to the primitive moth family Hepialidae, a group known as the ghost moths or swifts. Puriri Moth caterpillars initially feed underground on fine roots, and then move on to spend several years burrowing in the wood of a variety of trees.

# Confused Haploa

Tiger moths (formerly Arctiidae; now subfamily Arctiinae, family Erebidae, superfamily Noctuoidea) are usually boldly patterned moths that sometimes use both bright colors and clicking noises to warn predators such as bats that they are not good to eat. This brown and white Confused Haploa (*Haploa confusa*) is one of many common North American tiger moths. The bright orange tiger moth (*Rhipha flammans*, inset) was among dozens of different tiger moth species attracted to a night-light at a Costa Rican eco-lodge.

# Tiger Moth

The bright colors of tiger moths (subfamily Arctiinae) warn potential predators that they are protected by distasteful or toxic chemicals, usually sequestered from host plants but sometimes synthesized by the moth. Some tiger moths also advertise their bad taste by making ultrasonic clicks to deter bats, while others send a similar warning in the form of a bad odor. This Peruvian tiger moth is one of nine species of *Anaxita*, all restricted to the neotropics.

# Grote's Bertholdia

Tiger moths (subfamily Arctiinae) are favorites among moth collectors for obvious reasons, and the most colorful medium-sized moths attracted to night-lights are often in this family. These two, a Grote's Bertholdia (*Bertholdia trigona*) and a Painted Tiger Moth (*Arachnis picta*, inset) with the bright hind wings exposed, were attracted to a porch light in New Mexico.

# Wooly Bear

Many tiger moths (subfamily Arctiinae) are bright and familiar insects as both adults and larvae. One of the most well-known larvae is the boldly banded Wooly Bear (*Pyrrharctia isabella*), so often seen scurrying along in late fall as it seeks a place to spend the winter. The middle red band of Wooly Bear caterpillars varies in width, and folk wisdom suggests (incorrectly) that its width predicts the severity of the upcoming winter, with bigger bands predicting milder winters.

# Tiger Moth

These two pericopine tiger moths (*Hypocrita* sp., subfamily Arctiinae) were mating in broad daylight on an exposed leaf in the Bolivian rainforest. Such brazen behavior is probably explained by their arsenal of defensive compounds, including bitter chemicals such as pyrrolizidine alkaloids, that render these moths immune from most predators.

# Wasp Moth

Many different kinds of moths are mimics of stinging wasps, presumably gaining a level of immunity from attacks by sting-shy predators. Most wasp-like moths are either in the tiger moth group (subfamily Arctiinae) or in a small family of mostly root-boring moths called Sesiidae. This Costa Rican wasp moth (*Myrmecopsis ichneumonea*, subfamily Arctiinae) is such a good wasp mimic it was almost impossible to distinguish from co-occurring wasps in the field; only the mouthparts and antennae gave it away.

# Wasp Moth

Although it is a surprising habit for such delicate, clean creatures, many wasps and butterflies visit dung, carrion and urine in search of salts. This wasp moth (probably *Phoenicoprocta* sp., subfamily Arctiinae) has joined a couple of blowflies for a snack on a dead sloth in the Bolivian rainforest. Just as many male butterflies are frequently seen forming "puddle parties" in search of sodium, some butterflies and moths seek salt at less savory sites, such as scats or this stinking sloth.

# Zygaenid Moth

These zygaenid moths (*Pyromorpha centralis*, family Zygaenidae) are mating in the middle of the day in the Arizona desert, in full view of birds and other potential predators. They are protected not only by their close similarity to a very common and very bitter-tasting local beetle (a chemically protected net-winged beetle) but also by chemical defenses of their own. Bright colors advertising such defenses are called aposemetic colors; mimicry of one aposemetically colored insect by another well-defended species is called Mullerian mimicry, as opposed to Batesan mimicry, in which the mimic is only pretending to be unpalatable.

# Syntomid Moth and Net-winged Beetle



Although these two insects look remarkably alike and were photographed on the same day along the same Bolivian rainforest trail, one is a moth and one is a net-winged beetle (family Lycidae, inset). This is probably a case of mimicry, since Lycidae are brightly colored to warn predators that they are seriously nasty-tasting beetles, and many other insects use lycid-like shapes and colors to protect themselves from predation. The moth, *Correbidia notatabolivia*, is in a group of tiger moths known for imitating net-winged beetles.

# Owlet Moth

Pinned and spread moths (or pictures of pinned and spread moths) fail to reflect the distinctive shapes and poses of the living insects. These two common North American noctuoid moths (superfamily Noctuoidea) have spectacular features that disappear when they are pinned. The skinny *Palthis angulalis* (Erebidae) folds its wings longitudinally to get a sort of jet-fighter appearance; the common and robust *Autographa pseudogamma* (Noctuidae, inset) has thoracic tufts reminiscent of those on a ceremonial Roman helmet.

# Owlet Moth



As is true for many moths, this orange-banded *Sosxetra grata* (inset) and this green *Ceroctena amynta* (superfamily Noctuoidea, family Erebidae, subfamily Calpinae) are striking things to see in nature, even though these species look nondescript in collections of pinned moths. Both occur in South and Central America; the *Ceroctena* was photographed as it was pretending to be a necrotic spot on a leaf in the Bolivian rainforest, and the *Sosxetra* was found near an artificial light in Costa Rica.

# Prominent Moth

Prominent moths (family Notodontidae), so called because many species have a prominent tuft of hair projecting up from the front wing, are very similar to the more familiar owlet moths (family Noctuidae), another family in the large superfamily Noctuoidea. Most of the three or four thousand species of prominent moths are tropical (especially neotropical), like this *Crinodes besckei*. Although this photo was taken in Costa Rica, *Crinodes besckei* occurs from Mexico to Brazil and throughout the Caribbean.

# Slug Caterpillar

These two mobile mops, photographed in lowland rainforest in Bolivia, are slug caterpillars, the larvae of moths in the family Limacodidae (*Phobetron aquapennis* and a yellow *P. hipparchia*, inset). Similar species are known as hag moth caterpillars and monkey slug caterpillars.

# Crowned Slug

Slug caterpillars (family Limacodidae) are lovely to look at but painful to hold, because they are usually studded with urticating hairs or hollow, venom-filled spines. This Crowned Slug (*Isa textua*) is a common eastern North American species.

# Tropical Caterpillars

Tropical caterpillars seem almost endless in their variety of adornments, many of which either warn that the caterpillar is well-defended or are the defenses themselves. Spiky caterpillars like many giant silkworms (Saturniidae) are obvious untouchables but sometimes even the softest-looking caterpillars, like the aptly named flannel moths (Megalopygidae), are armed with venom-loaded spines that break off on contact with your skin, with unpleasant results. These caterpillars are from Bolivia; the orange one (inset) is in the family Megalopygidae.

# Tarchon Caterpillar

The colorful and richly clothed Tarchon caterpillars or shag carpet caterpillars (family Apatelodidae, sometimes treated as part of the Bombycidae) are so spectacular that a *Prothysana felderi* (= *Tarchon felderi*) was recently featured on a Panamanian postage stamp. The *Tarchon* caterpillars shown here are from Venezuela and Ecuador (inset).

# White-lined Sphinx Moth



Most sphinx moths (family Sphingidae) are crepuscular, hovering over pale flowers in the gloom of early night while they seek nectar with their long, coiled proboscis. A few, however, are day-active, and it is not unusual to see hummingbird moths (*Hemaris* spp.) and White-lined Sphinx moths (*Hyles lineata*) hovering over flowers in broad daylight. The White-lined Sphinx (here over a purple flower) is widespread, but this photo is from New Mexico.

# Domestic Silkworm Moth

This domestic silkworm moth (*Bombyx mori*, family Bombycidae) has just emerged from its pupa hidden within its protective silken cocoon. The newly emerged moth used salivary secretions (spit) to dissolve the silk at one end of the cocoon, turning the silk brown while softening up an escape route. Silkworm cocoons reared for the silk industry are killed before the adult emerges; the white cocoon is unwound into a strand of silk almost half a mile long.

# Giant Silkworm Moth



Many moths are inconspicuous when at rest with the hind wings concealed but can show a flicker of color by abruptly flashing the hind wings when disturbed. That seems to be the case for this *Gamelia* (family Saturniidae) found on the Bolivian forest floor following an overnight storm.

# Giant Silkworm Moth

*Hyperchiria nausica*, a giant silkworm moth (family Saturniidae) that ranges from Mexico to South America, is a remarkable dead-leaf mimic while at rest (inset) but shows a startling pair of eyespots when it exposes its hind wings. Researchers have shown that birds are effectively frightened off when suddenly presented with paired-eye images—no doubt a generally adaptive response for the bird, but effectively capitalized upon by many moths.

# Bloodshot-eyed Moth



The aptly named Bloodshot-eyed Moth (*Syssphinx hubbardi*) is a relatively small member of the giant silkworm moth family (Saturniidae). This one was photographed in New Mexico—about the middle of the species' southwestern American range—where it develops on leaves of acacia and mesquite.

# Gypsy Moth

This female Gypsy Moth (*Lymantria dispar*, family Lymantriidae) is laying eggs in a matrix of chopped silk that will insulate her eggs until they hatch in the following spring—unless tiny parasitic wasps come along and lay their eggs inside the moth eggs. Gypsy Moths were introduced to North America, and their larvae, such as this mature caterpillar on a tree trunk (inset), defoliate a variety of trees.

# Douglas Fir Tussock Caterpillar



In some years the larvae of Douglas Fir Tussock Moths (*Orgyia pseudotsugata*, family Lymantriidae) are tremendously abundant, and these tufted caterpillars can do significant damage to fir forests. The Douglas Fir Tussock Moth is considered a significant pest in western North America, even though numbers are kept under control naturally by a nucleopolyhedrosis virus that causes periodic population crashes.

# Chain-dotted Geometer

This Chain-dotted Geometer (*Cingilia catenaria*) is sticking her eggs to the underside of a blueberry leaf. This species is associated with peatlands and heaths in eastern North America, where it can be locally abundant, although the species can be rare on a statewide or province-wide basis. The Chain-dotted Geometer is a protected species in Massachusetts.

# Inchworm



Larvae of moths in the family Geometridae are called inchworms because they are missing the middle abdominal legs and walk by "looping" or "inching." This brightly banded inchworm (*Pseudasellodes fenestraria*) was feeding on a Costa Rican shrub in the coffee family (*Randia armata*, family Rubiaceae). Its bright colors suggest that it is an inedible species, protected by toxic chemicals picked up from its host plant. Moths in the family Geometridae, like this unidentified adult moth from Bolivia (inset), usually sit flat against foliage or tree trunks and are often very difficult to see. This one resembles a fragment of lichen-spattered bark and would have been all but invisible against another background.

# Swallowtail Moth

Swallowtail moths in the genus *Urania* (family Uraniidae) are day-flying moths with a remarkable similarity to swallowtail butterflies. There are only four *Urania* species; *Urania lailus* is common in the Amazon Basin, where it feeds on lianas (vines) in the family Euphorbiacae. This one was photographed on wet mud along the shore of an Amazon tributary in Peru.

# Snout Moth

Snout moths (family Pyralidae) are so called because of the mouthparts (labial palps), which form distinctive snouts. The two snout moths shown here are grass moths (subfamily Crambinae) with snouts that really stick out, especially the bottlebrush-like schnoz on the duller of these two species (*Agriphila ruricolella*). These tiny moths are common but easily overlooked inhabitants of eastern North American meadows.

# Cosmopterygid Moth

Caterpillars of this pretty micromoth (*Euclemensia bassettella*, family Cosmopterygidae) live hidden away inside the shells of female scale insects (*Kermes* spp.) on oak trees; adult moths emerge from the hardened dead scales through an opening cut by the larva.

# Planthopper and Parasitic Caterpillar



Almost all moths develop on plant material, but a few are scavengers and a very few develop as parasites of other animals. Members of the family Epipyropidae are external parasites that attach themselves to planthoppers. This Bolivian planthopper (inset) is being consumed alive by a waxy white epipyropid caterpillar (normally hidden under its wings).

# Yucca Moth

Yucca moths (family Prodoxidae), such as this *Tegeticula yuccasella* inside a yucca flower in a Canadian garden, are entirely dependent on yucca flowers for larval development. Yucca flowers are in turn entirely dependent on yucca moths for pollination.

# Urodus Moth

This unusual moth (*Urodus* sp., now in family Urodidae but previously in family Yponemeutidae) has just emerged from a cocoon suspended from a leaf by a silken thread; the moth is still clinging to the cocoon and the pupal skin can be seen sticking out of the top of the silken cocoon. This is a Bolivian species, but the genus ranges north to United States.

# Caddisfly

Adult caddisflies (order Trichoptera) are moth-like insects that have hairy wings rather than the scaly wings of similar small moths (order Lepidoptera). These inconspicuous, nocturnally active insects usually stay near the ponds, lakes and streams in which their larvae develop. The net-spinning caddisfly (*Parapsyche*, family Hydropsychidae) shown here is from eastern North America, but most caddisfly adults are remarkably similar the world over.

# Finger-net Caddisfly

This finger-net caddisfly (*Chimarra* sp., family Philopotamidae) is emerging from its mobile pupa, which has just climbed out of a cold Canadian stream. Caddisflies pupate underwater in silken shelters or cocoons, usually leaving their shelter by cutting through the silk with scissor-like mandibles and then swimming and crawling to the surface with long-fringed legs. The pupal mandibles and legs are operated like a puppet by the adult inside the pupa, which is really a "pharate adult."

# Caddisfly

Caddisfly larvae are fabulously diverse, but most use salivary silk to make some sort of shelter, net or case. Species that make portable tube-like cases occur in the widest variety of aquatic environments and take on every shape imaginable, ranging from snail shells and log cabins to flat sand disks. The caddisfly larvae shown here is the widespread but uncommon North American *Fabria ornata* (family Phryganeidae), which makes its tube from long bits of vegetation assembled in a spiral construction.

# Fishfly

Dobsonflies and fishflies (family Corydalidae) usually lay their eggs in masses on hard objects over flowing waters. The eggs fall into the water and hatch into predaceous larvae (inset) with solid, well-muscled mandibles. This Canadian fishfly (*Nigronia serricornis*) is laying her eggs under a concrete bridge.

# Dobsonfly

The distinctively greenish yellow dobsonflies in the genus *Chloronia* occur throughout Central and South America, where their larvae are common predators in running water. Dobsonfly adults are generally nocturnal, and the best way to find them is to watch artificial lights near rivers or streams.

# Dobsonfly

Dobsonfly (family Corydalidae) males in the genus *Corydalis*, such as this one that came to the lights at a Costa Rican cloud-forest lodge, have huge crossed mandibles. The predaceous larvae, known as hellgrammites, develop in rivers and streams.

# Antlion

Larvae of the most common antlions make conical pits in the sand, which they use to trap ants and other small insects that they suck dry through long, sickle-like mouthparts. Larvae of this Chilean antlion (family Myrmeleontidae) have similar mouthparts and similar predaceous habits, but instead of making pits in the sand they conceal themselves among the spiny leaves of *Puya chilensis*, a terrestrial bromeliad (the plant this adult is resting on) found on the arid hillsides of Chile.

# Owlfly



This adult owlfly (family Ascalaphidae, order Neuroptera) is striking a characteristic resting pose with its abdomen stuck up like a short twig on a tree in the Bolivian rainforest. Owlflies have been described as the neuropteran equivalent of dragonflies, since the adults are active, strong-flying predators, unlike the slow-flying adults of most other Neuroptera. The larvae look much like antlion larvae and prey on other insects, which they impale with their long, sickle-shaped mandibles. This larva (inset) was found in a crevice of a dead eucalyptus tree in Australia.

# Osmylid Lacewing

Nerve-winged insects (order Neuroptera) in the family Osmylidae are found almost all over the world but are absent from North America. Larvae (inset) have remarkably elongate mandibles that are used to probe streamside mosses for midge larvae and other insects. Like those of all members of the order Neuroptera, the mandibles are hollow and serve as pointed straws for consuming the contents of prey.

# Brown Lacewing

This brown lacewing (*Gayomyia* sp., family Hemerobiidae) from Robinson Crusoe Island in the Juan Fernandez Islands, Chile, reacts to disturbance by retracting its legs and antennae and dropping to the leaf litter, effectively disappearing among similar-looking bits of dead leaves.

# Green Lacewing

Green lacewings (family Chrysopidae, order Neuroptera) are predators as both adults and larvae; the larvae are so voracious that the eggs are deposited on stalks so the first larva to hatch cannot easily devour its siblings. Both this decorated adult and these spirally deposited eggs (inset) are from the Bolivian rainforest.

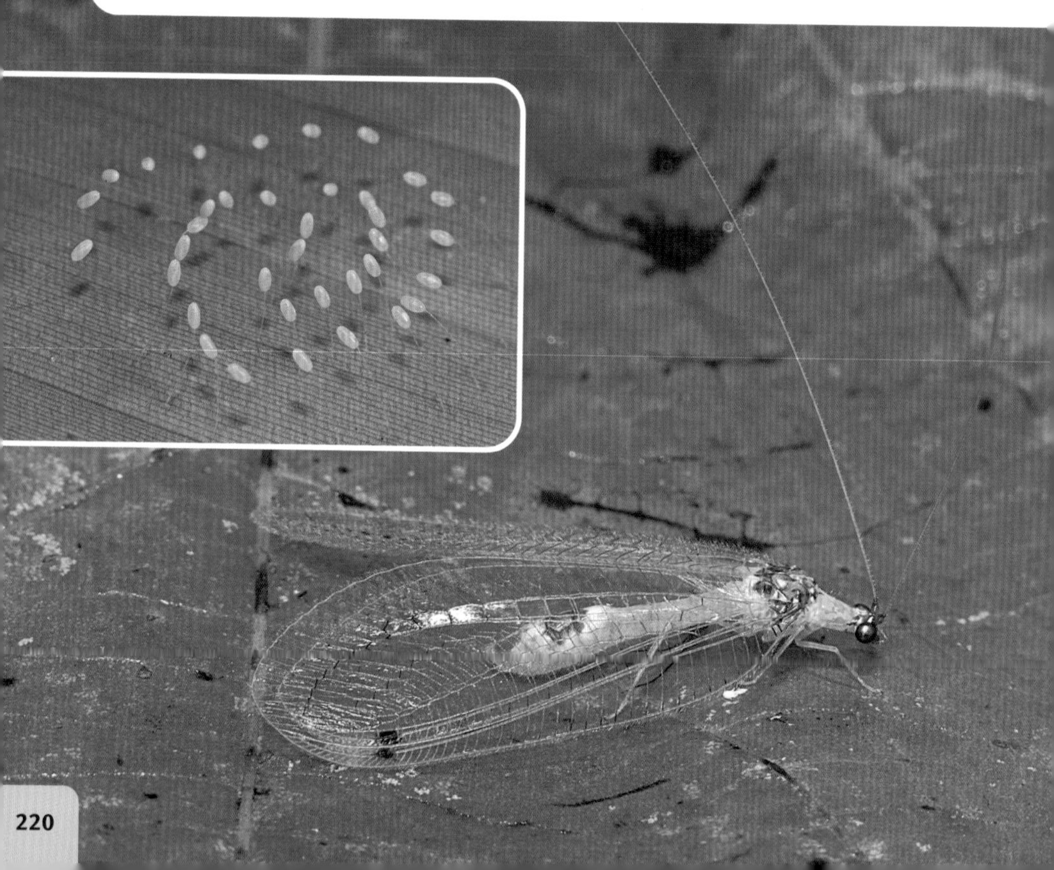

# Mantisfly



Mantisflies (family Mantispidae) are neither flies nor mantids; rather, they are members of the order Neuroptera with mantis-like forelegs that the adults use to capture small prey. Most larval mantisflies in the typical subfamily Mantispinae live inside the egg sacs of spiders, in some cases after hitching a ride on an adult female spider. Hitchhiking larvae use their syringe-like mouthparts to suck the blood of adult spiders prior to becoming egg-suckers, if they are lucky enough to invade an egg sac. Mantisflies are widespread; this *Climaciella semihyalina* is from Bolivia. Many mantisflies are striking mimics of stinging wasps.

# Ground Beetle

Ground beetles (family Carabidae) in the genus *Ceroglossus* are common insects of the southern beech (*Nothofagus*) forests of south and central Chile. These variably colored predators can be found under logs during the day, although at night they roam the leaf litter in search of prey. It is best not to handle them with your bare hands since, like many ground beetles, they produce pungent defensive secretions in glands near the tip of the abdomen.

# Ground Beetle



Despite the common name "ground beetles," some Carabidae spend their lives well off the ground, and members of the genus *Calophaena*, like this Ecuadorian beetle, live only on the broad leaves of *Heliconia* plants.

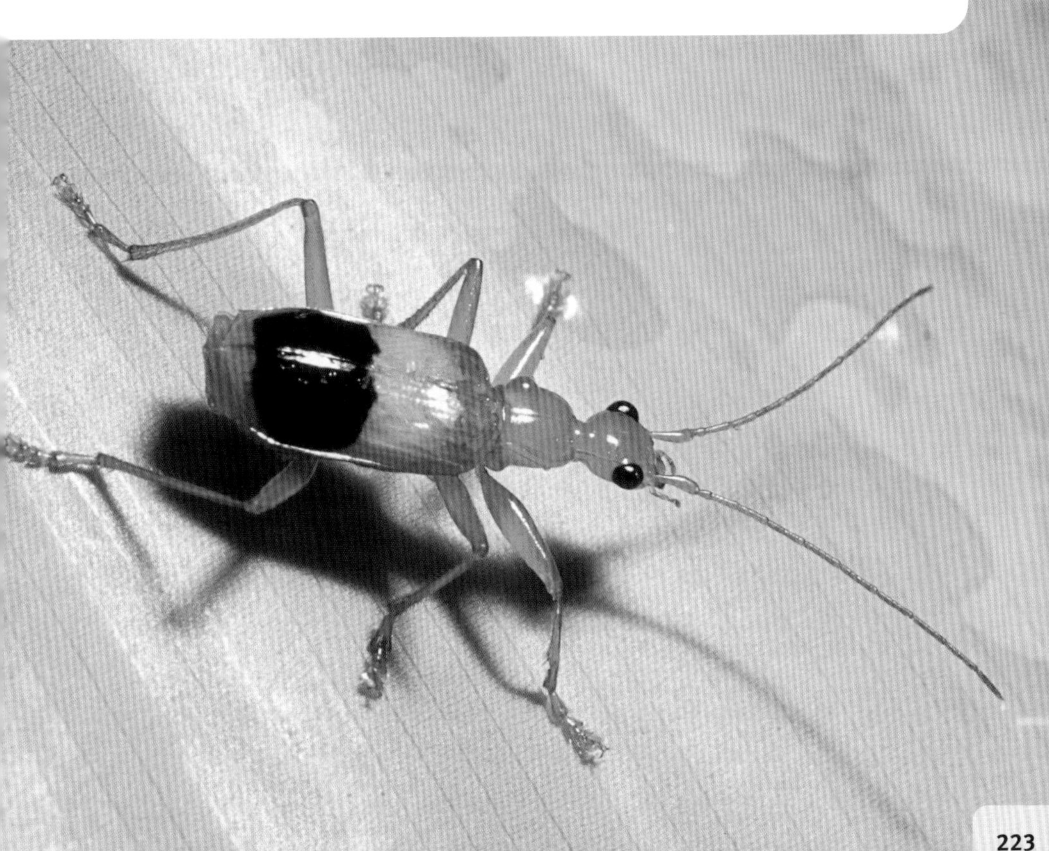

# Ground Beetle

This ground beetle (*Trichognathus marginipennis*, family Carabidae) is munching up the remains of an insect captured along a South American river. Some similar ground beetles are known as bombardier beetles because of their penchant for popping potential predators with a hot chemical punch mixed up in a reaction chamber at the tip of the abdomen.

# Tiger Beetle

Tiger beetles (family Cicindelidae or subfamily Cicindelinae, family Carabidae) are mostly day-active visual predators, but members of the genus *Tetracha* (previously treated as part of *Megacephala*) are nocturnal hunters. Like other tiger beetles, *Tetracha* adult males exhibit a behavior known as mate-guarding. This Bolivian male is holding on to a female with his large jaws, defending his reproductive investment by protecting his mate from other males.

# Tiger Beetle

Tiger beetles in temperate zones usually live on the ground, often choosing particular types of open surfaces such as sand or clay from which to launch ambush attacks on passing insects. Tropical tiger beetles, including members of the neotropical genus *Odontocheila*, such as this Bolivian beetle, are more likely to be arboreal insects that hunt from tree leaves.

# Western Red-bellied Tiger Beetle



Tiger beetles (subfamily Cicindelinae) are common predators, easily seen stalking prey with their big eyes and big jaws during daylight hours. The male of this Arizona pair of Western Red-bellied Tiger Beetles (*Cicindela sedecimpunctata*) is using his big jaws to guard his mate, protecting his paternal investment. Tiger beetle larvae are big-headed predators that live in burrows and feed by lunging partway out of their burrows to grab passing prey.

# Whirligig Beetle

Whirligig beetles (family Gyrinidae), such as this *Andogyrus ellipticus* from Chile, are marvelously adapted to literally straddle the water surface. Unlike water striders and other insects that walk on top of the surface film, whirligigs spend their water-surface time half in the air and half in the water. The upper and lower parts of the body each have a separate pair of eyes, and the dish-like antennae sit in the surface film to detect waves indicating the presence of potential prey such as drowning terrestrial insects. Whirligig larvae are aquatic predators.

# Burrowing Water Beetle

Burrowing water beetles (family Noteridae) are found around the roots of vascular aquatic plants. The larvae puncture the stems or roots to obtain oxygen, effectively using the plants as living snorkels. This strikingly convex species is *Suphis inflatus*, from the southeastern United States.

# Riffle Beetle

Riffle beetles (family Elmidae) such as this *Stenelmis quadrimaculata* from eastern Canada are slow-moving grazers found on vegetation, rocks and woody debris in flowing water. Unlike most other adult insects, riffle beetles don't have to surface periodically to replenish their air supplies, because they have a plastron, a permanent bubble of air, held in place by millions of fine hairs. The plastron, seen as areas of silvery surface, serves as a permanent gill that allows oxygen to be drawn from the surrounding water.

# Rove Beetle



This rove beetle (*Rugilus fragilis*) was photographed in eastern Canada but, like so many organisms now common in North America, it is an accidental European import. Rove beetles produce an exceptional arsenal of complex defensive chemicals in glands near the tip of their elongate abdomen, and some should not be allowed to touch your skin.

# Rove Beetle

This is one of dozens of individuals of *Nordus fungicola* that arrived at an ephemeral soft fungus on a cloud-forest log in Costa Rica. These relatively large (up to 0.6 inch/1.5 cm in length) fungus-eating rove beetles (family Staphylinidae) fly conspicuously around rotting fungi during the day, frequently landing on the fungi or nearby vegetation.

# Fly-trapping Rove Beetle

Fly-trapping rove beetles (*Leistotrophus versicolor*, family Staphylinidae) feed on adult flies, which they usually ambush as they arrive at decomposing materials (this beetle was photographed in an Ecuadorian compost heap). In the absence of natural rotting materials to attract their prey, these flexible rove beetles manufacture "perfumes" to lure in small flies. The beetle's fly bait is produced at the abdominal tip; to attract flies the beetle either waves its abdomen tip with its scent-releasing devices or deposits the bait on leaves or rocks, then positions its massive mandibles over the fly-attracting material.

# Rove Beetle

The distinctively short-winged rove beetles (family Staphylinidae) are usually predators, but some members of this incredibly diverse group (almost 50,000 species worldwide) feed on fungi. This predaceous *Glenus* from Bolivia has struck a typical rove beetle pose on a leaf, holding up its flexible abdomen and prominently exposing an abdominal tip loaded with a formidable arsenal of defensive chemicals.

# Rove Beetle

This black and orange rove beetle (*Plociopterus* sp., family Staphylinidae) has just landed on a leaf in the Bolivian rainforest and elaborately folded its large, membranous hind wings, which are now tucked away under its very short, hairy forewings (elytra). Like most other rove beetles, this is a predaceous species.

# Myrmecophilous Rove Beetle

Foraging columns of the New World army ant *Eciton hamatum*, seen here returning from a raid on the nest of another ant species, are frequently infiltrated by other insects that run with the raiders and often behave much like their ant hosts. The skinny beetle making like a member of this ant column is a myrmecophilous rove beetle (*Ecitophya* sp, family Staphylinidae). The many species of myrmecophilous, or ant-associated, beetles are either predators or scavengers in ant nests.

# Glorious Beetle

The aptly named Glorious Beetle (*Chrysina gloriosa*) is inconspicuous among the juniper leaves on which it feeds, but this one is gloriously bright against an Arizona tree trunk. These southwestern scarabs (subfamily Rutelinae, family Scarabaeidae) frequently fly to lights. As in all scarabs, the antennae have clubs made of lobes, or lamellae, that can fold up out of the way.

# Beyer's Scarab

The famous golden scarabs of Central America belong to the genus *Chrysina*, a mostly neotropical group with almost a hundred species ranging from the southern United States to northern South America. Costa Rica is a center of golden scarab diversity, with 22 species that include the silvery beetles hand-held in this picture (inset). Members of this group range from brilliant gold to bluish, metallic red and various shades of green such as in this Beyer's Scarab (*Chrysina beyeri*) in Arizona. Although conspicuous in hand, these shimmering beetles are inconspicuous against the foliage on which they feed; larvae usually develop in rotting wood. Adults are rarely seen in their natural habitat but often show up around lights at night.

# Scarab Beetle

The ends of the antennae of scarab beetles (family Scarabaeidae) are asymmetrically expanded into broad lobes, or lamellae, providing extensive surfaces for the sensory structures that help these beetles locate appropriate places to lay their eggs. The antennal lamellae on this Chilean *Oryctomorphus macullicolis* (subfamily Rutelinae) are spread apart, but scarabs can also close their lamellae to form a compact club.

# Shining Leaf Chafer

The family Scarabaeidae (scarab beetles) is best known for its dung-feeding habits, even though most members of the family feed on plant material that has not yet been digested by vertebrates. Shining leaf chafers, such as these *Brachysternus prasinus* from Chile, belong to a scarab subfamily (Rutelinae) in which adults feed on foliage and fruit while larvae eat roots.

# Shining Leaf Chafer

Some shining leaf chafers (subfamily Rutelinae, family Scarabaeidae), such as this *Lagochile amazona* from Bolivia, are among the most brilliantly metallic of all insects. Adults usually feed on fruits and larvae feed on roots; a few of the 4,100 or so species in the subfamily feed on cultivated plants, and a very few species are pests.

# Flower Scarab Beetle

This Australian *Glycyphana* belongs to a group of scarab beetles (subfamily Cetoniinae) known as the flower scarabs because they frequent flowers, where they feed on pollen. Larvae of most flower scarabs are found in decaying materials, although a few develop in ant nests. Many species are associated with particular flowers and sometimes appear for brief periods as conspicuous and abundant flower visitors.

# Manuka Beetle



During the spring months the Manuka Beetle (*Pyronota festiva*) is a tremendously common scarab beetle (subfamily Melolonthinae) in the high country of New Zealand. Although their host plant, manuka, is rich in defensive oils, these abundant beetles must be palatable, because they are snapped up by trout when they blow or blunder into nearby streams. They are imitated by a variety of bright green fishing flies popular among Kiwi anglers.

# American Rhinoceros Beetle

The American Rhinoceros Beetle (*Xyloryctes jamaicensis*, subfamily Dynastinae, family Scarabaeidae) is an impressively chunky beetle over an inch (2.5 cm) long that gets its common name from the long, upright head-horn sported by the male. Males use their horns to force other males away from contested resources such as females or feeding and egg-laying sites; females have only a small tubercle rather than a horn. These beetles develop in dead wood and compost heaps.

# Scarab Beetle

Scarab beetles in the subfamily Scarabaeinae typically stock their underground nests, or burrows, with dung in which their larvae develop. *Sulcophanaeus* species, such as this *S. velutinus* from Costa Rica, make "feeding burrows" that they stock with sausage-shaped masses of dung. They later use the dung to make "brood balls"—balls of dung coated with soil—in nearby burrows; larvae develop in these carefully constructed and sequestered balls of poop.

# Dung-rolling Scarab Beetle

Dung-rolling scarabs (subfamily Scarabaeinae, family Scarabaeidae) usually lay their eggs in dung. They compete with other insects seeking this hotly contested resource by carving a chunk off the mother lode and rolling it far away, where it is further sequestered in an underground burrow. Dung-rollers, such as this small *Canthon luteicollis* from Bolivia, have their hind legs situated far back on the body to help them stay in control of the ball while moving backwards.

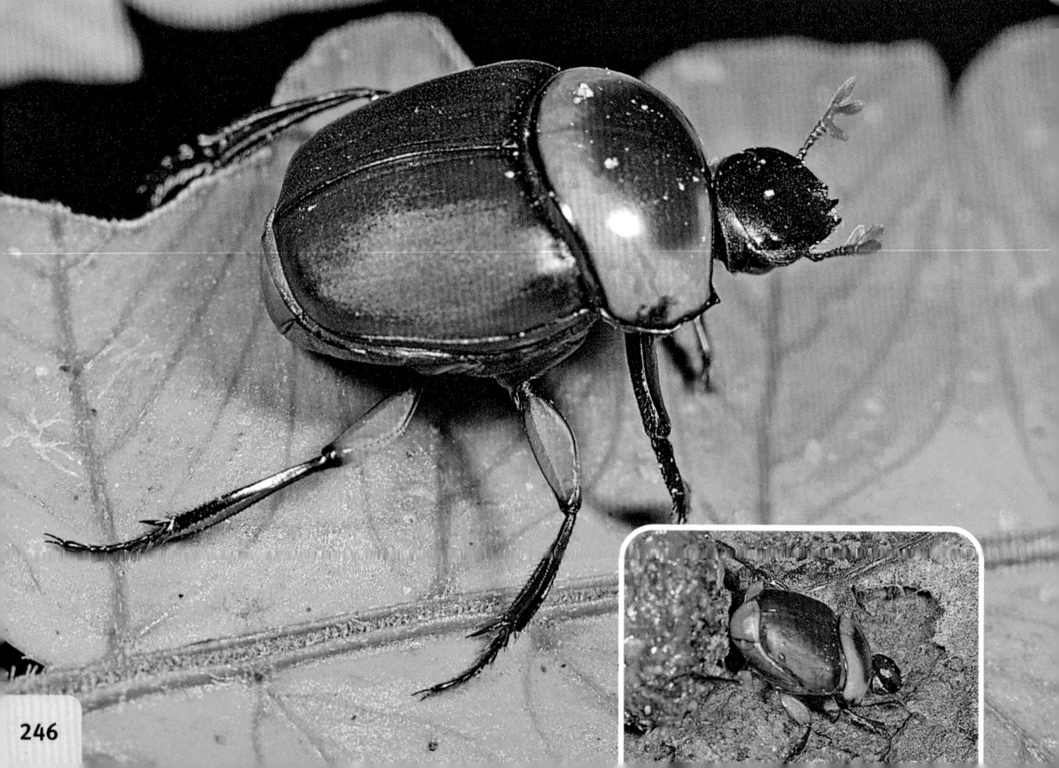

# Scarab Beetle



Although this massive *Coprophanaeus* (*Megaphanaeus*) belongs to the dung-rolling scarab subfamily Scarabaeinae, it was found on the body of a long-dead sloth in the Bolivian rainforest. Most Scarabaeinae are normally dung-rollers, but a few feed on other decomposing material ranging from vertebrate carrion to dead invertebrates. Despite the generic name, which implies coprophagous (dung-eating) habits, *Coprophanaeus* species are normally attracted to carrion rather than dung.

# Dung Beetle

*Oxysternon conspicillatum* is a massive (about 1 inch/2.5 cm) beauty that is easy to collect in lowland forests through much of South America merely by putting out one of its favorite foods—human dung. These spectacular dung beetles (subfamily Scarabaeinae, family Scarabaeidae) are likely to plop promptly right into any "bait" you deposit in the forest.

# Golden Stag Beetle



Stag beetles, such as this Golden Stag Beetle (*Lamprima aurata*) from Australia, are favorites among insect collectors—so much so that there is a flourishing trade in stag beetle specimens and "livestock." Members of this family (Lucanidae) are distinctive for the male's long mandibles (giving rise to the name) and their lobed antennae. Unlike the similar antennae of scarabs, the lobed antennal club of stag beetles cannot be closed up into a ball. These harmless beetles normally develop in dead wood.

# Texas Soldier Beetle

Soldier beetles (family Cantharidae) are common visitors to flowers worldwide, and species of the genus *Chauliognathus* are found almost everywhere. The Texas Soldier Beetle, *Chauliognathus scutellaris*, is one of 19 North American species in the genus. The scientific name for soldier beetles implies mighty mandibles (*chaulio* is Greek for impressive; *gnathus* is a common Greek suffix referring to "jaws" or mouthparts), but these soft-winged predaceous or pollen-feeding beetles are neither particularly soldier-like nor impressively jawed.

# Soldier Beetle

This *Chauliognathus lecontei* (family Cantharidae) was among dozens frenetically mating and pollen-feeding as they flew in and out of a small patch of seepwillow (*Baccharis glutinosa*). The beetle's bright colors warn predators that these conspicuous insects are inedible; if attacked, they pump milky, foul-tasting defensive chemicals out of paired glands on the thorax and abdomen.

# Firefly

Fireflies (family Lampyridae), like the superficially similar net-winged beetles, are unpalatable beetles that make no attempt to conceal themselves. Adults of this common North American species, *Lucidota atra*, are day-active; they lack the bioluminescent organs for which other (mostly nocturnal) adult fireflies are famed. The larvae, however, like all firefly larvae, are bioluminescent.

# Firefly



Firefly (family Lampyridae) larvae are often active hunters of both aquatic and terrestrial snails; this larval *Pyractomena borealis* has buried its head in a mollusc victim's shell on a southern Ontario tree trunk. Larval fireflies invariably glow, and even the pupae, such as this pink *Pyractomena* pupa (inset), are bioluminescent. Even though not all adult fireflies have luminescent organs, the conspicuous displays of species-specific bioluminescence of some mate-seeking adult fireflies (including *Pyractomena*) give the family its well-known name.

# Ceiba Borer

Adult Ceiba Borers (*Euchroma gigantea*, family Buprestidae) are common in the rainforests of Central and South America, where they are familiar for their unusually large size (2.5–3 inches/6.4–7.6 cm), noisy daytime flights and conspicuous landings. Larvae are borers in several kinds of fallen trees, including the ceiba and balsa common in the Bolivian forest where this one was photographed.

# Jewel Beetle

The widespread jewel beetle genus *Polycesta* includes some of the prettiest Buprestidae in several parts of the world, including Australia, the western United States, Madagascar and Chile. This is *Polycesta costata*, a common wood-boring beetle in Chile.

# Jewel Beetle

Beetles in the family Buprestidae, such as this *Psiloptera torquata* from Cuba, are aptly called jewel beetles because of their often brilliantly metallic, rock-hard bodies. Larvae, called flat-headed wood borers, usually bore into the phloem tissue under the bark of trees.

# Jewel Beetle

All jewel beetles (family Buprestidae) in Western Australia, such as this black and yellow *Castiarina*, are protected species, and it is illegal to collect them. Large and attractive insects like jewel beetles and stag beetles are so sought after by some collectors that they can command high prices on the international market. This sets the stage for unscrupulous collecting by commercial dealers who could potentially damage populations of rare species, even though insect collecting normally has no appreciable impact on insect populations. The other beetle in this picture is a long-horned wood borer (family Cerambycidae).

# Jewel Beetle

Jewel beetles in the genus *Acmaeodera*, such as these *A. solitaria* mating and eating pollen on an Arizona flower, resemble many conspicuous flower-visiting insects in having wasp-like black and yellow colors. *Acmaeodera* species enhance their wasp mimicry by leaving the elytra—the hard front wings that give beetles their characteristic folding armor—closed when flying, giving them an amazingly wasp-like appearance in flight. Most beetles hold their elytra outstretched during flight, but *Acmaeodera* and one group of bee-like scarabs are able to fly by popping their hind wings out of notches at the base of the closed elytra.

# Jewel Beetle

One of the most conspicuous beetles of the southwestern American deserts, this jewel beetle, *Gyascutus caelata*, is a common insect. It draws attention to itself not only because of its large size (often more than 1 inch/2.5 cm) but also with its loud buzz as it flies between acacia bushes.

# Jewel Beetle

This beetle using its telescoping abdominal tip to lay eggs in the trunk of a New Zealand tree is *Nascioides enysii*, one of only two native New Zealand species in the jewel beetle family (family Buprestidae, also known as metallic wood borers). Jewel beetle larvae usually bore under the bark or in the wood of trees.

# Blister Beetle

Blister beetles (family Meloidae) such as this *Megetra* from New Mexico are slow-moving insects that are usually protected from predators by toxic body fluids that they release from their leg joints ("reflex bleeding") if attacked. Most potential predators avoid blister beetles, but cantharidin, the protective chemical synthesized by these beetles, is not enough to put off some desert insect eaters. Horned lizards, apparently, are undeterred by prey literally oozing with cantharidin.

# Blister Beetle

Blister beetles (family Meloidae), such as this brightly colored Costa Rican *Cissites auriculata*, are among the most interesting of all beetles, not only for their famous blistering defensive chemicals but also for their remarkable life cycle. Young larvae are active, long-legged forms that seek out a host such as a bee or a grasshopper egg mass. Older larvae become fat and immobile squatters in the host's nest or egg mass.

# Blister Beetle

Blister beetles (family Meloidae), such as this ghostly white Costa Rican *Epicauta isthmica*, are so named because they produce a nasty defensive chemical, cantharidin, that can cause painful blistering if it touches your skin. Males of these otherwise soft and apparently defenseless beetles produce large quantities of defensive compounds, which are transferred to the female during mating.

# Blister Beetle

This three-striped blister beetle is one of several almost identical *Epicauta* species found in the southwestern United States. *Epicauta* species hatch from eggs as active larvae that hunt for grasshopper egg masses, where they settle down and transform into fat, relatively immobile larvae feeding on the hopper eggs. Other blister beetles hatch into active larvae that latch on to bees at flowers, riding back to the bee's nest, where they develop in the stored pollen.

# Nuttall's Blister Beetle



Nuttall's Blister Beetle (*Lytta nuttalli*) is a distinctive western North American blister beetle (family Meloidae) in the same genus as the famous Spanish Fly. The Spanish Fly, a European species of *Lytta* (*L. vesicatoria*), is the source of the supposed aphrodisiac of the same name: a powder made of crushed beetles that contains enough of the beetle's blistering defensive chemical (cantharidin) to be a serious health hazard if applied to human tissue.

# Wedge-shaped Beetle

Beetles in the family Rhipiphoridae are parasitoids of bees and wasps. The beetle larvae latch on to their hymenopteran hosts as they visit flowers, clinging to the winged wasps and bees until they return to their nests. Larvae of this rhipiphorid species, *Macrosiagon limbatum*, hitch rides back to the nests of solitary wasps, where they parasitize the wasp larvae. Females have simple antennae, unlike the feathery antennae of this male.

# Soft-winged Flower Beetle

Soft-winged flower beetles are often conspicuous flower visitors, where they can play an important role in carrying pollen from plant to plant. The large (0.5 inch/1.2 cm) *Astylus trifasciatus* is probably the most common flower-frequenting beetle in Chile. This variably colored species has been known under a dozen different species names.

# Red Yucca Checkered Beetle

The Red Yucca Checkered Beetle, *Enoclerus spinolai* (family Cleridae), is one of 36 North American species in this genus of brightly colored predators. *Enoclerus* species usually hunt down beetle larvae in confined spaces such as wood borings. This beetle was munching weevil larvae between the leaves of an Arizona yucca.

# False Ladybird Beetle

False ladybird beetles are strikingly convex tropical beetles usually found among fungi on mossy logs or trees. This small group of 40 or so species is sometimes treated as the family Nilionidae and sometimes as the subfamily Nilioninae of the family Tenebrionidae.

# Darkling Beetle

Darkling beetles (family Tenebrionidae) are incredibly diverse in size and shape, ranging from 0.04 to 3.2 inches (0.1–80 cm). Most of the 20,000 or so world species are found in dry or desert areas, and many, such as this red-legged Chilean *Epipedonota* (inset), and this dark-legged southwestern American *Glyptasida*, are conspicuously active on open ground, where they are protected from predators by a combination of tough armor and potent glandular secretions.

# Darkling Beetle

The 130 or so species in the darkling beetle genus *Eleodes* (family Tenebrionidae) are familiar and conspicuous beetles in the western United States, so much so that they are known under several common names, including stink beetle, circus beetle, skunk beetle and headstander beetle. The latter name reflects a habit shown here, of raising the tip of the abdomen to spray or exude volatile and stinky defensive chemicals. Some desert mice bypass the beetle's defense by grinding its tail-end chemical factory into the ground before munching away from the head down.

# Click Beetle

Most of the thousands of species in the large click beetle family (Elateridae) have a similar distinctive streamlined shape with sharply pointed "shoulders," and all have a click mechanism made from a spine that crosses under the main articulation in the beetle's body and snaps into a groove on the other side. The click or snap can propel an upside-down beetle into the air far enough to do a couple of somersaults and startle most potential predators. This red and black beetle is the aptly named *Elater ruficollis* from Chile, a species named by Linnaeus in 1758.

# Lady Beetle

Many members of the worldwide lady beetle family Coccinellidae are "beneficial" predators that have been moved between countries as potential biological control agents against aphids, scales and related pests. This South American species, *Eriopis connexa*, for example, was imported to the United States and released for biological control of the exotic Russian wheat aphid, *Diuraphis noxia*. It is probably fortunate that the release was a failure, since exotic predators often create more problems than they solve. The beetle in this picture is a Chilean subspecies, *E. connexa chilensis*.

# Seven-spotted Lady Beetle

Seven-spotted lady beetles, *Coccinella septempunctata*, are European in origin but have become secondarily widely distributed as we have deliberately carried them around the world to help us in our battles against pest aphids. Both adults (like this one) and larvae of most red and black lady beetles eat aphids.

# Convergent Lady Beetle

This crush of copulating Convergent Lady Beetles, *Hippodamia convergens*, was part of a large aggregation among mullein foliage near the top of a mountain in Arizona. In some areas this widespread species migrates to high elevations to form large seasonal aggregations in which mating takes place. The aggregations can be so large and dense that it is commercially viable to harvest lady beetles from their mountain hibernacula for sale elsewhere.

# Lady Beetle

These two South Pacific lady beetles (family Coccinellidae) are common in New Zealand and Australia; the bright reddish and black Variable Lady Beetle (*Coelophora inaequalis*) is now becoming common elsewhere as it is moved around for the biocontrol of aphid pests. This one was photographed on the Cook Islands, but the same species is now spreading through the southern United States following its recent deliberate introduction to Florida. The black and yellow lady beetle (inset) seen here on top of another lady beetle pupa is the Fungus Eating Lady Beetle (*Illeis galbula*), so called because it is one of the several lady beetles that grazes mold off leaf surfaces.

# Ironclad Beetle

Ironclad beetles (part of the family Zopheridae), like this *Zopherus tristis* walking on the sizzling sands of the Imperial Dunes in southern California, are arguably the toughest insects on the planet. Ironclad beetles are sometimes used as living jewelry in Mexico, decorated with beads and attached to jewelry to serve as mobile adornments on shirts or blouses. They are virtually crush-proof and impenetrable (try sticking an insect pin through one!), and they can survive for long periods without food or water.

# Pleasing Fungus Beetle

Look closely at the top of this pleasing fungus beetle (*Aegithus burmeisteri*, family Erotylidae) munching on a bit of fungus growing on a fallen tree in the Bolivian rainforest. The five little insects perched on the beetle's back are scelionid wasps waiting for the beetle to lay eggs, which will serve as hosts for these little parasitoids.

# Pleasing Fungus Beetle

Some of the most in-your-face beetles, conspicuous because of both their bright colors and exposed habits, are the pleasing fungus beetles, or Erotylidae. This orange species (*Ellipticus gemellatus*) was near a fungus-covered log along a Costa Rican forest path. Pleasing fungus beetle larvae and adults usually feed on the fruiting bodies of fungi, although some feed in mycelia or in mycorrhizal associations with tree roots.

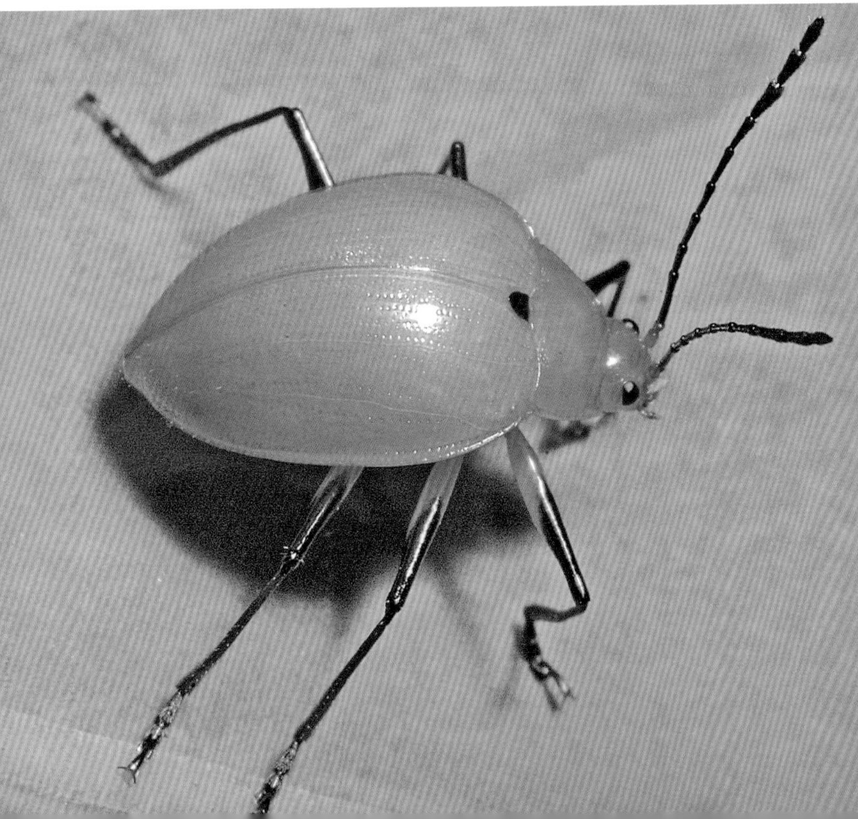

# Pleasing Fungus Beetle

The Erotylidae (pleasing fungus beetles) are a diverse family of about 2,300 species found all over the world, although most species are tropical and only 50 or so occur in North America. This luridly colored Costa Rican species, *Gibbifer gibbosus*, was found feeding on fungi in the middle of the day, but many other species come out of hiding only during the night.

# Pleasing Fungus Beetle

*Gibbifer californicus* (family Erotylidae) is a common beetle in the American southwest, especially at higher elevations. This larva (inset) and this mating pair are feeding on fungi. Other members of the genus *Gibbifer* are found in the New World tropics.

# Pleasing Fungus Beetle

This orange and black pleasing fungus beetle (*Erotylina maculiventris*, family Erotylidae) is feeding on fungus on a fallen tree in the Bolivian rainforest. These brightly colored beetles are probably, like most warningly colored insects, inedible.

# Pleasing Fungus Beetle



Pleasing fungus beetles (family Erotylidae) such as this *Mycotretus duodecimguttatus* from Bolivia are often brilliantly and conspicuously colored. Although usually associated with fungi, they are often seen on foliage or fallen trees.

# Handsome Fungus Beetle

This pair of handsome fungus beetles (*Corynomalus* sp., family Endomychidae) was picked out by flashlight in the middle of a Bolivian rainforest. Many beetles, especially fungus-feeding beetles, are active at night, and beetle hunting with a light is always productive on warm nights with high humidity.

# Handsome Fungus Beetle

Handsome fungus beetles (family Endomychidae) in the genus *Corynomalus* (previously *Amphix*) are common insects of South and Central America. Clusters of *A. cincta* adults are often found grazing fungi on dead wood along with their peculiar humpbacked larvae (inset).

# Harlequin Beetle

The Harlequin Beetle, *Acrocinus longimanus*, is one of the most widely recognized and widespread of neotropical insects, occurring on a variety of trees from Mexico to Argentina. Males, which have extraordinarily long front legs, stridulate by scraping the front of the thorax against the wing covers. The larvae of these huge long-horned beetles (family Cerambycidae) bore in the trunks of various kinds of fungus-infested tropical trees.

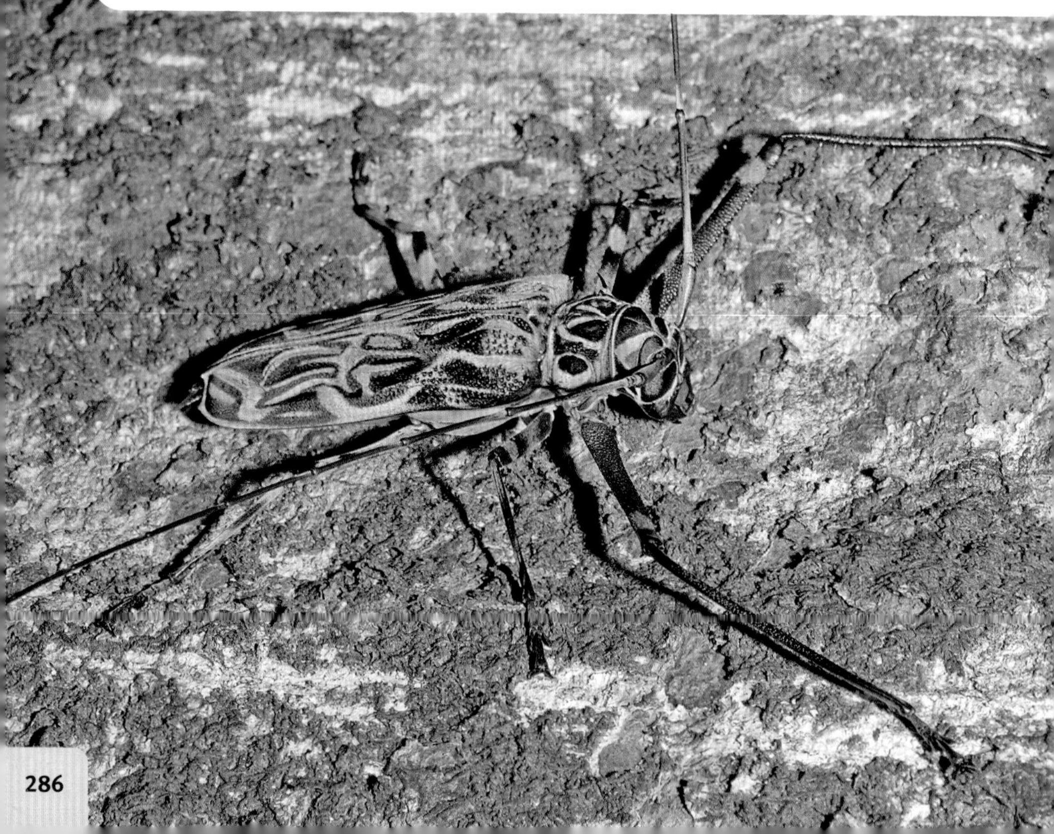

# Cactus Longhorn Beetle

Cactus longhorn beetles (*Moneilema* spp.) are robust long-horned beetles of the family Cerambycidae that sometimes bear an uncanny resemblance to inedible desert darkling beetles (page 271). As the name suggests, they eat cactus plants—this adult *M. gigas* is eating the outside of a cactus pad near Tuscon, Arizona; five other species occur in deserts of Mexico and the American southwest. Larvae feed from inside the cacti, entering through the roots. The similarity between cactus longhorns and inedible desert darkling beetles extends to behavior: the long-horned beetles imitate toxic tenebrionids by standing on their heads when threatened, implying that they exude poisons like similar headstanding darkling beetles (they don't).

# Long-horned Beetle

Wild rose flowers are great places to look for pollen-feeding insects such as these two long-horned beetles (family Cerambycidae). Both this brightly marked *Evodinus monticola* and the relatively drab *Grammoptera subargentata* belong to a subfamily called the flower longhorns, which are commonly seen munching on pollen as adults and found boring under bark as larvae.

# Long-horned Beetle

Many insects, especially in the tropics, are superbly camouflaged through their similarity to leaves, buds or twigs. This Bolivian long-horned beetle (*Ecthoea quadricornis*, family Cerambycidae) looked so much like a twig that I had to pick it off and put it on a leaf (inset) to convince myself it was indeed a beetle.

# Leaf Beetle

This colorful Leaf Beetle from Cuba, *Neolema dorsalis*, belongs to a group of leaf beetles (subfamily Criocerinae) in which the larvae make protective shelters from their own feces. Some *Neolema* larvae incorporate toxic chemicals from their host plants into their fecal shields, using the plant's defense to repel predators and parasitoids.

# Flea Beetle

Flea beetles such as these Bolivian species are leaf beetles (family Chrysomelidae) that earn their common name by making Herculean leaps with conspicuously swollen, muscular hind legs. Adult flea beetles often make small holes in plant foliage, giving it a shotgun-blasted appearance. This distinctive group of leaping leaf beetles has traditionally been treated as the subfamily Alticinae but is now treated as part of a larger subfamily, Galerucinae.

# Leaf Beetle

The leaf beetle family Chrysomelidae is an enormous group of more than 35,000 species, most of which feed on only one or a few kinds of plants. This host specificity has evolved because most plants have different defensive chemicals, and the leaf beetles that feed on them have had to develop different specialized ways to bypass or detoxify those defenses. Some leaf beetles go a step further and sequester the plants' defensive chemicals for their own use, often advertising the fact with bright colors to deter predators. This Bolivian *Stilodes* is in the same subfamily (Chrysomelinae) as the Colorado Potato Beetle, another brightly colored beetle that obtains defensive compounds from its host plant.

# Leaf Beetle

Leaf beetles in the enormous tropical genus *Platyphora* (subfamily Chrysomelinae, family Chrysomelidae) obtain a complex variety of protective chemicals from their host plants, advertising their toxicity with conspicuously bright colors. Some *Platyphora* have a dual chemical defense, producing different defensive compounds from different chemicals sequestered from host plants. This gaudy, slow-moving species was photographed in the Peruvian Amazon.

# Tortoise Beetle

These aptly named tortoise beetles are Bolivian species in the large leaf beetle subfamily Cassidinae. Like other tortoise beetles, they can shelter their head and antennae below a tortoise-like shell (*Coptocycla dolosa*, inset) made by the expanded elytra and pronotum. Many species are brilliantly metallic in life but lose their colors as they dry out in death; some have a chameleon-like ability to change color while alive.

# Target Beetle

This is the Target Beetle, *Ischnocodia annulus*, a common beetle found from Argentina north to Mexico. Like other tortoise beetles (subfamily Cassidinae, family Chrysomelidae), the Target Beetle can hide its head and legs under an expanded shell made from the margins of the elytra and pronotum; on this individual you can see the head and appendages through the transluscent shell. Larvae feed on plants in the families Boraginaceae and Lauraceae.

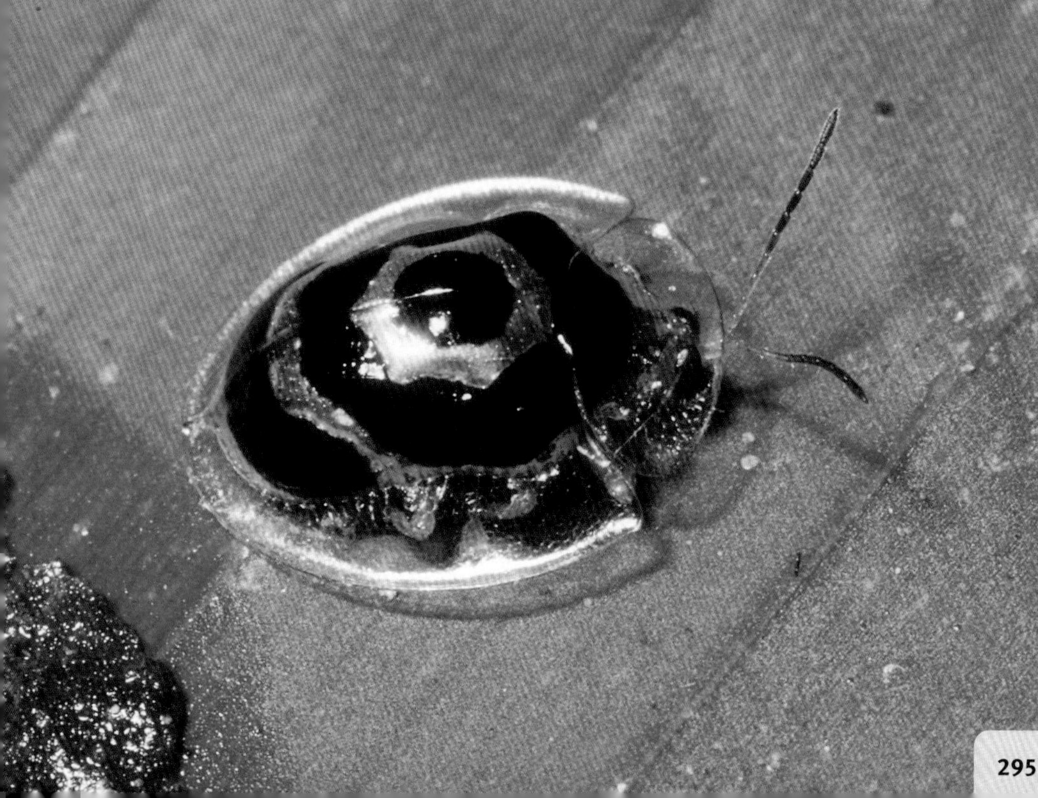

# Clavate Tortoise Beetle

Although tortoise beetles are most conspicuously diverse in the tropics, they are also common insects in temperate regions. The Clavate Tortoise Beetle, *Plagiometriona clavata*, abounds on nightshades and other common weeds in the tomato family (Solanaceae) throughout eastern North America. Like other larvae in the subfamily, larvae of the Clavate Tortoise Beetle use their "tail" to hold a sort of protective parasol covered with feces over the body (inset). Since many tortoise beetles feed on the foliage of toxic plants (including most Solanaceae), this tacky, toxic tail deters most would-be predators.

# Tortoise Beetle

Some of the largest tropical tortoise beetles belong to the genus *Stolas*, which has some 178 species, including this Costa Rican species. Tortoise beetle eggs are heavily parasitized by tiny wasps, especially those from the family Eulophidae, and some parasitic wasps hang out on female beetles waiting for a chance to attack her eggs. Look closely at the right side of this orange-spotted Costa Rican *Stolas* for a parasitic wasp.

# Arizona Tortoise Beetle

Tortoise beetles in the distinctive genus *Physonota* are widespread beetles with host specializations reflected in their common names, such as Sunflower Tortoise Beetle (*P. helianthi*) and Horsemint Tortoise Beetle (*P. unipunctata*). These beetles mating on a ragweed plant in Arizona belong to a geographically restricted species aptly called the Arizona Tortoise Beetle (*Physonota arizona*). Many related species occur in Mexico.

# Tortoise Beetle

These convex, strikingly tortoise-like tortoise beetles are obviously capable of hunkering down under their shells and resisting predators. Both this metallic green species (*Hybosa insculpta*) from Bolivia and this red Costa Rican *Spaethiella miniata* (inset) were found in tropical forests abounding in ants. Similar hemispherical tortoise beetles can pull their shells down so tightly it takes much more force than an ant can apply to pry them up. Some species cling to leaf surfaces with feet covered in thousands of tiny forked hairs and oily secretions that stick them down so tightly the pull needed to detatch them is nearly 60 times the beetle's weight. Other species cling to surfaces using large claws at the end of their feet.

# Tortoise Beetle

Some so-called tortoise beetles, such as this odd-looking *Aslamidum* from Bolivia, seem to have characteristics in common with both tortoise beetles and leaf-mining beetles. Larvae of *Aslamidum* and related genera feed on foliage like tortoise beetle larvae, but they live in rolled or appressed leaves, hidden away like leaf-mining beetles. Their characteristic feeding damage has been recognized in 66-million-year-old fossil ginger leaves, showing that this group of beetles not only coexisted with dinosaurs, they outlived them. The tortoise beetles (Cassidinae) and the leaf-mining beetles (Hispinae) are closely related and are now often treated as a single subfamily.

# Leaf-mining Leaf Beetle

Leaf-mining leaf beetles (subfamily Hispinae, family Chrysomelidae), such as these *Microrhopala vittata* on a Canadian goldenrod, have strikingly flattened larvae that develop between the upper and lower surfaces of leaves. The adults don't mine leaves but they do inherit a flat shape from their larvae. Leaf-mining leaf beetles are very closely related to the tortoise beetles, so closely that many scientists include tortoise beetles in the same subfamily as the leaf-mining beetles.

# Cholus Weevil

This Bolivian weevil, a member of the huge genus *Cholus*, is clinging to the surface of a leaf with the tarsal pads of its middle and hind legs. In all weevils, as well as the related long-horned and leaf beetles, the third tarsomere (tarsal segment) of each leg is greatly expanded and more or less heart-shaped, forming huge pads covered with tiny hooked hairs that help them cling to shining leaf surfaces. The fourth tarsomere is tiny, hidden between the lobes of the third tarsomere, while the fifth bears large tarsal claws.

# Burrito Weevil

The rock-hard, slow-moving weevils in the genus *Aegorhinus* sometimes go by the common name *burritos* in their native Chile, where their larvae feed on the bark and main roots of various trees, including planted hazelnuts. The weevil family (Curculionidae) includes more than 50,000 species, making it the largest family of living things.

# Flower Weevil

Weevils in the tribe Baridini (subfamily Conoderinae) are known as flower weevils because members of this group are fairly common on flowers, especially Asteraceae, in North America. This spectacularly spined species, *Pteracanthus smidtii*, however, was photographed as it flew from leaf to leaf in a Costa Rican rainforest. This distinctive neotropical species was first named by Fabricius, a student of Linnaeus, the father of modern taxonomy, more than 200 years ago. It is so unlike other weevils that it was later put in its own genus, and it remains the only species of *Pteracanthus*. The long thoracic spines are probably used by males to fight with each other over females, as in similar weevils in the subfamily Conoderinae.

# Fly Weevil

This big-eyed *Macrocopturus* weevil is perched on a fallen tree, but it would disappear like a shot if approached too closely, since it belongs to a large subfamily of weevils (Conoderini, until recently known as subfamily Zygopinae) that move more like nervous flies than other beetles. Some members of the group really do look like flies and are thought to be active fly mimics. Larvae of this species probably develop in dead wood, but some members of the genus, such as the Mahogany Bark Weevil, *M. floridanus*, damage living trees.

# Fly Weevil

Males of some weevils in the fly weevil tribe Conoderini (subfamily Conoderinae), such as these *Hoplocopturus* from Costa Rica, fight for females on particular leaves or parts of broad leaves. Dozens of males can often be seen squaring off very briefly for bits of prime turf as other males and females swiftly fly in and out of the "arena."

# Agave Weevil

Although most members of the so-called fly weevil subfamily Conoderinae are neotropical, the Agave Weevil, *Peltophorus polymitus*, is a common insect from Mexico to the American southwest. It uses its prominent beak to perforate the leaves of agave plants, including *Agave lechuguilla*, one of the most characteristic plants of the Chihuahuan desert; larvae live inside agave stems.

# Fungus Weevil

This garish, elephant-snouted Ecuadorian beetle is a fungus weevil (family Anthribidae) in the mostly tropical American genus *Gymnognathus*. Despite the common name fungus weevil, this species probably develops in the twigs and branches of fallen trees such as the one under this beetle. Many other fungus weevils do feed on fungi, especially hard fungi.

# Straight-snouted Weevil

This Bolivian straight-snouted weevil (family Brentidae) has mandibles at the end of a long snout, as in true weevils (family Curculionidae), but it lacks the elbowed antennae of true weevils. Straight-snouted weevils occur throughout the world, and the slow-moving adults are frequently seen clinging to twigs or bark on or around recently cut rainforest trees. Larvae are usually wood borers. The family Brentidae includes not only the characteristically shaped straight-snouted weevils but also some dissimilar but closely related smaller weevils such as the enormous genus *Apion*, which includes the familiar Hollyhock Weevil.

# Austral Weevil

Belid weevils (family Belidae), also known as Austral weevils in recognition of their virtual restriction to Australia, form a peculiar group of weevils that lack the elbowed antennae of true weevils (family Curculionidae). As in true weevils, the adult mandibles are at the end of a snout and the larvae are fat grubs that live in plant material, usually inside stems and branches. Also like true weevils, belid weevils will fold their legs and drop to the ground and play dead when disturbed. This is *Rhinotia suturalis*, a species common around Brisbane, Australia.

# Scorpionfly

Scorpionflies are so named because males of common scorpionflies (family Panorpidae), such as this *Panorpa lugubris* on a South Carolina goldenrod flower, have genitalia that look like a scorpion's sting. Other families of scorpionflies have less conspicuous genitalia, but most are nonetheless distinctive for their long snouts that end in chewing mandibles used to munch on living or dead insect prey.

# Hanging Scorpionfly

Scorpionflies often have complex mating behavior, and males may court or occupy mates using "nuptial gifts" such as the captured insect being consumed by the female of this pair of Western Australian *Harpobittacus* (left). Hanging Scorpionflies (family Bittacidae) like *Harpobittacus* and this North American *Bittacus* (right) form a widespread group of long-legged scorpionflies that hang from the vegetation by their long front legs while using the long terminal claws on their other legs to grab insect prey.

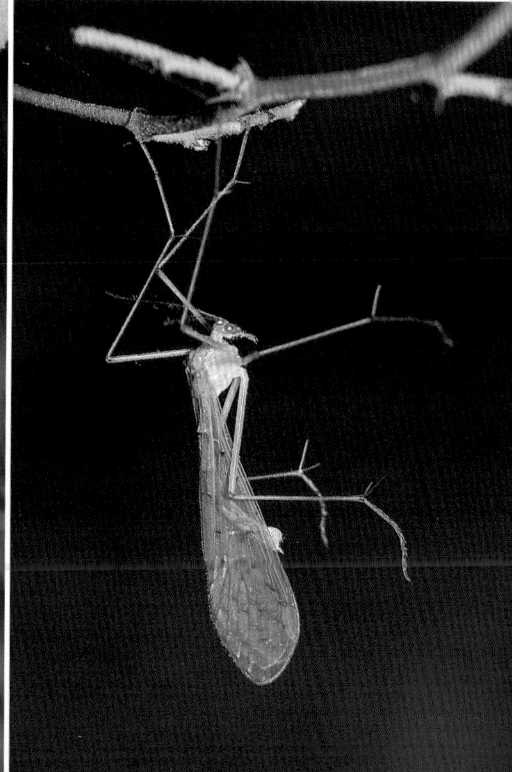

# Net-winged Midge



Members of the family Blephariceridae are sometimes called net-winged midges because of the intricate meshwork of fine creases on their wings. They are also called torrent midges because the aquatic larvae look like living suction cups stuck to rocks in rushing rivers or cascading mountain creeks. The single larva shown (inset) here is surrounded by black fly (family Simuliidae) larvae in a Chilean stream, and this adult net-winged midge is nectaring on a flower alongside the same stream.

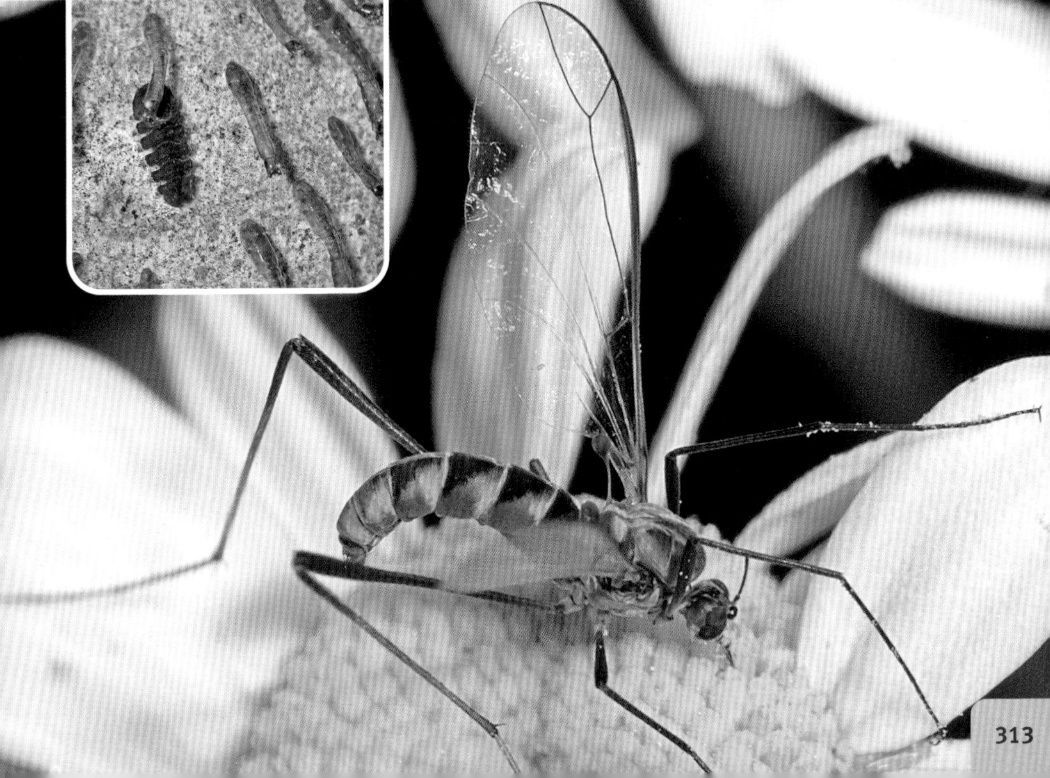

# Crane Fly

Crane flies in the genus *Ctenophora* (named for the comb-like male antennae) are among the most colorful species in the huge family Tipulidae, a worldwide family of long-legged flies with more than 14,000 species. Female *Ctenophora dorsalis*, like the black and orange member of this Canadian couple, have an unusually long and robust abdominal tip to help them lay eggs in dead wood.

# Crane Fly

This brightly colored *Tipula nobilis* is an eastern North American species of crane fly (family Tipulidae), but species of the enormous and diverse genus *Tipula* develop in a wide variety of terrestrial and aquatic habits and habitats throughout the world. The most commonly encountered species develop underground, where they feed on the roots of plants.

# Phantom Crane Fly

Phantom crane flies (*Bittacomorpha clavipes*, family Ptychopteridae) are often momentarily glimpsed as they slowly drift through the air among wetland plants, improbably suspended by tiny wings that are dwarfed by the fly's long, outstretched legs. Part of the leg is swollen and full of air tubes that assist the floating flight of these phantasmic flies. Larvae live in the muck in the bottom of shallow flowing waters, breathing through a long, snorkel-like tube projecting from the end of the body like the tail of a rat. Phantom crane flies are widespread; this *B. clavipes* was photographed in northern Ontario.

# Gall Midge

Gall midges (family Cecidomyiidae) are arguably the least known of all insects. About 5,000 species of these minute, fragile flies have been formally named, but recent estimates suggest that there could be as many as 20,000 species in Costa Rica alone. This group of flies was clustered among hundreds of other flies on a few leaves in a Costa Rican cloud forest.

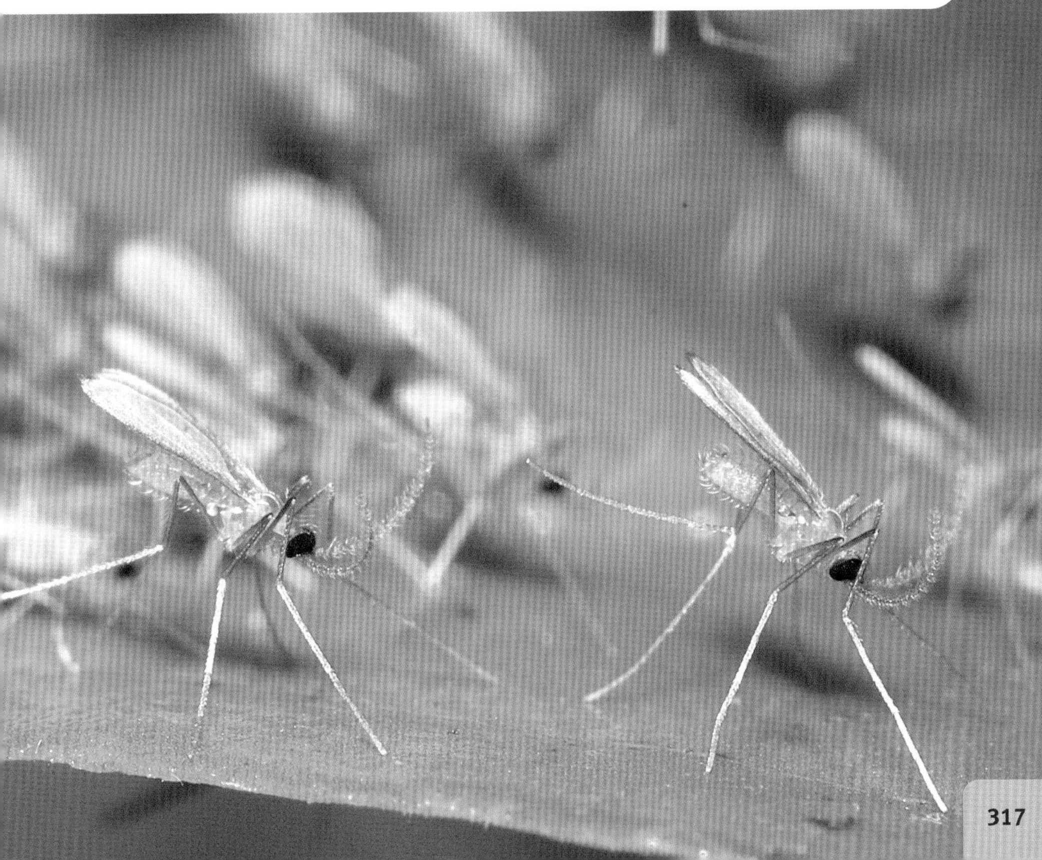

# Gall Midge

Hanging out in spider webs seems like a foolish thing for a fly to do, but several lineages of tiny flies in the diverse family Cecidomyiidae do just that, and often in impressive numbers. These rows of midges were swinging from spider silk in Arizona and New Mexico, but similar behavior has been observed all over the world. It seems unlikely that the web-maker doesn't notice the flies as they dangle from silken threads, but perhaps these minute creatures are not worth a spider's effort, and perhaps their seemingly dangerous perch gives them protection from other predators and parasitoids.

# Midge

About half of all aquatic insects belong to a single huge family of tiny midges, the Chironomidae. These are the ubiquitous little flies that swarm near ponds, lakes and rivers and throng artificial lights on midsummer nights. Males usually have big, feathery antennae, unlike the females. Larvae are found in all kinds of aquatic or semiaquatic habitats; some common species that abound in low-oxygen environments contain hemoglobin, giving them a bright red color (inset).

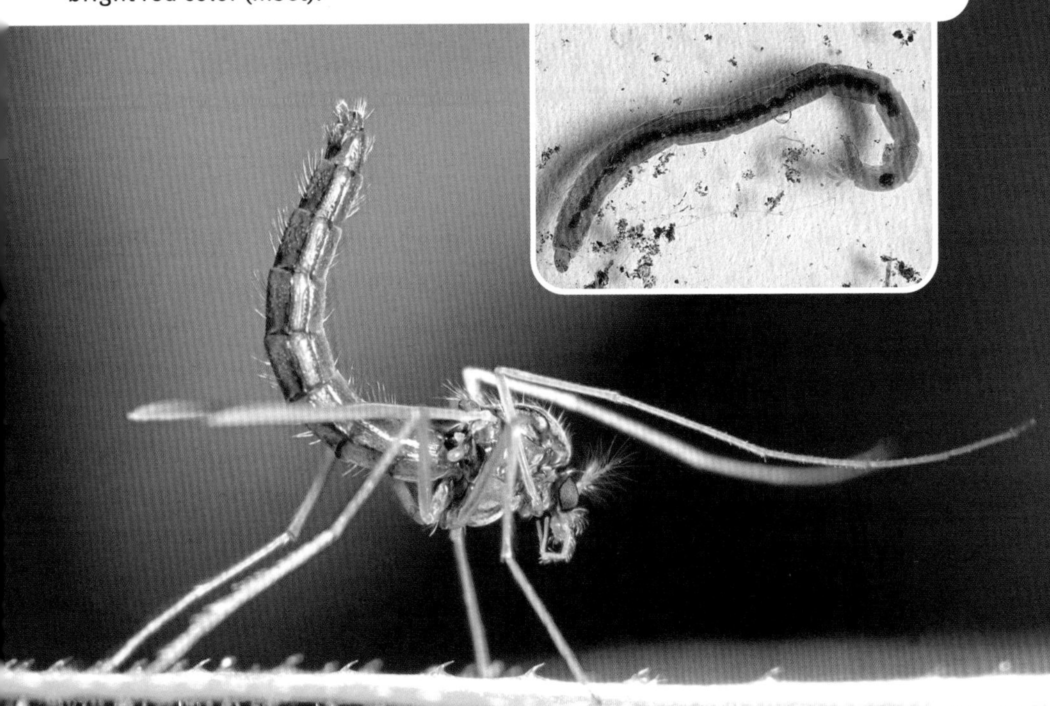

# Sand Fly

This little *Lutzomyia* was photographed in a cave in Cuba, where it lurked on the damp walls awaiting an opportunity to imbibe blood from a visiting vertebrate. Members of this subfamily of Psychodidae (Phlebotominae) are called sand flies. Some (*Lutzomyia* in the neotropics and *Phlebotomus* in the Old World) can transmit disease-causing microorganisms, particularly a dangerous protozoan that causes leishmaniasis, when they bite people.

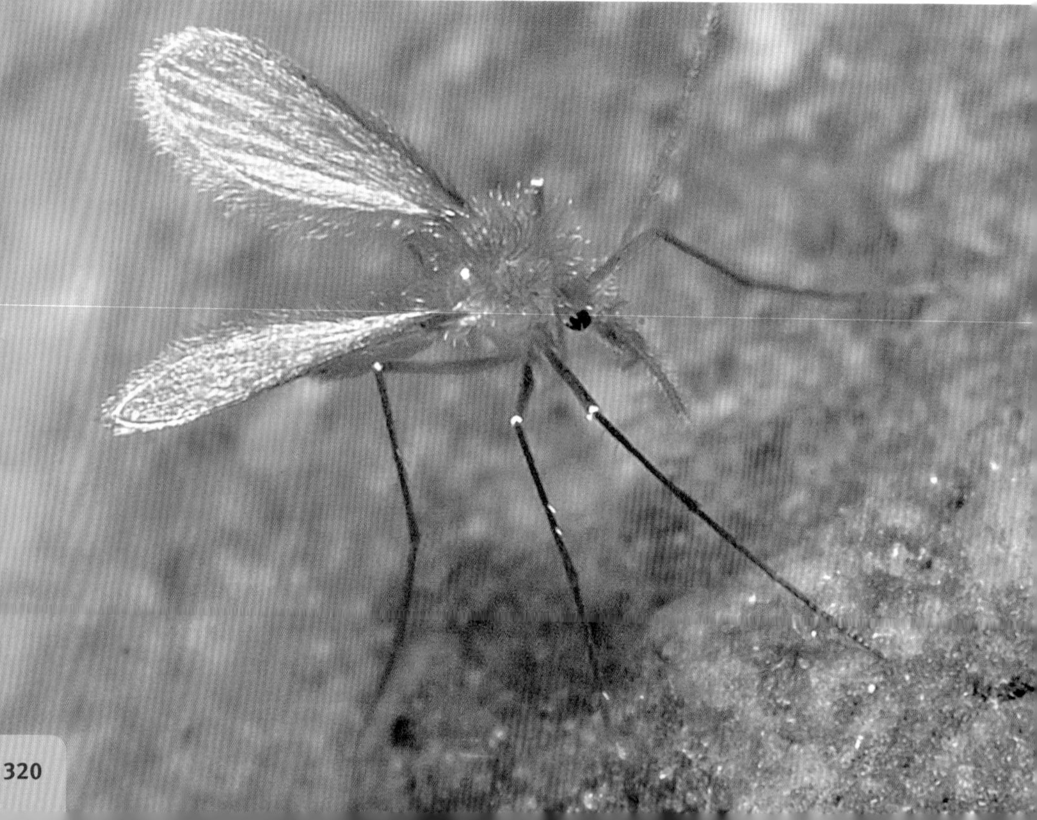

# Moth Fly



Moth flies (family Psychodidae) are aptly named little flies that look much like minute moths. Some can be found as close as the nearest public washroom, almost anywhere in the world, where their larvae live in the goo found deep in most drains. Others, such as this minute white fly photographed in the Costa Rican rainforest, are delicate beauties known only from remote and wild places.

# Black Fly

Black fly larvae live only in flowing water, where they can anchor their fat bottoms to the substrate by hooking themselves to silk pads that they spit out where they want to hang on. Once anchored they can let the flow buffet them as they filter food out of the current, using two big, net-like or fan-like structures that extend from their upper lip (labrum). The fans can be folded back through the mouthparts to transfer the food to the mouth. Adult females of some black flies feed on vertebrate blood; this Chilean species (inset) is among the relatively few that attack humans.

# Malaria Mosquito

This pretty fly, photographed among hundreds of similar flies on my window screen after a sleepless night in a Central American jungle cabin, belongs to the most deadly genus of insect—*Anopheles*. Although this species (*Anopheles neivai*) is fairly harmless, other *Anopheles* species are the only carriers of malaria, arguably the world's most important disease.

# Treehole Mosquito

Giant treehole mosquitoes (*Toxorhynchites* spp.) are not blood feeders, apparently getting all the protein they need as predaceous larvae feeding on other mosquito larvae in tree holes. Neither males (with the feathery antennae, inset) nor females bite, as is fairly evident from the distinctively downcurved proboscis. *Toxorhynchites* mosquitoes are common in Central and South America (this one is from Bolivia), but rare along the northern fringe of their range in southern Canada.

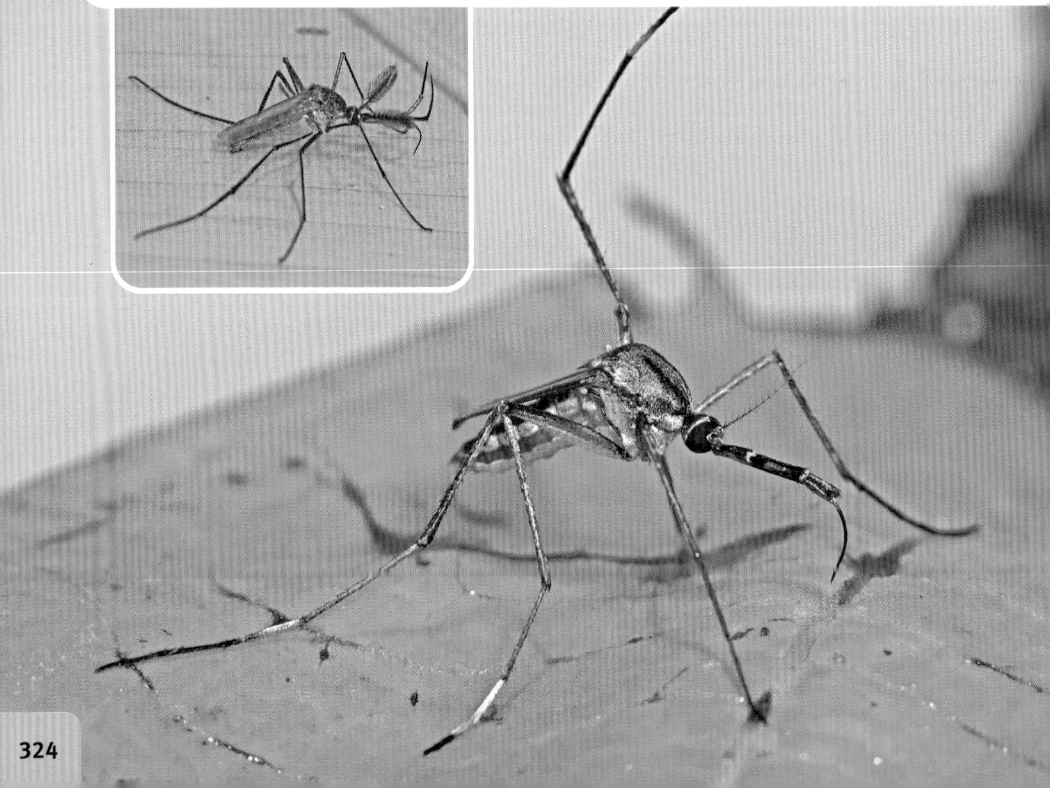

# Mosquito

Most biting mosquitoes in the Amazon Basin belong to relatively few species of the genera *Aedes* and *Psorophora*, like this pretty *Aedes* (*Ochlerotatus*) *fulvus* hanging out under a leaf and this female *Psorophora* (inset) resting on top of a leaf after getting a bellyful of my blood.

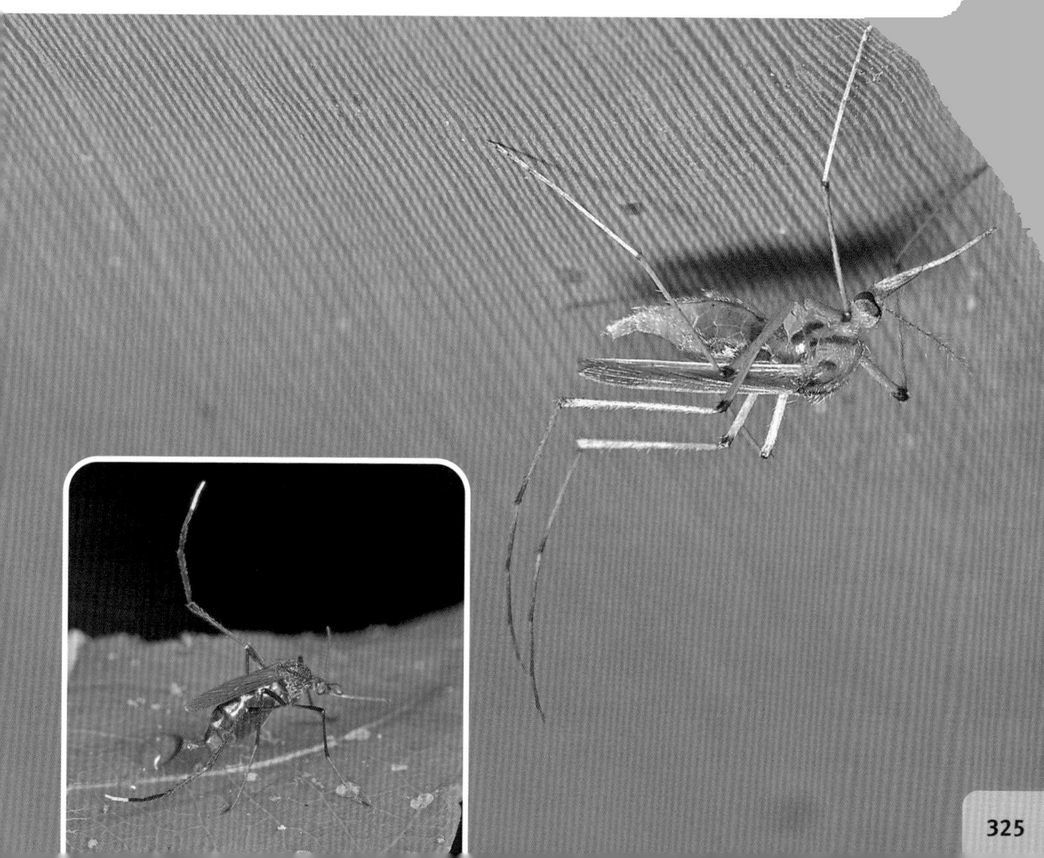

# Sapphire Mosquito

This exotic-looking mosquito belongs to a species that is rarely noticed because of its small size and innocuous habits (they only bite leeches and worms!), even though it ranges from Mexico north to Canada. The species name *Uranotaenia sapphirina* aptly describes the sapphire blue scales that adorn parts of the body.

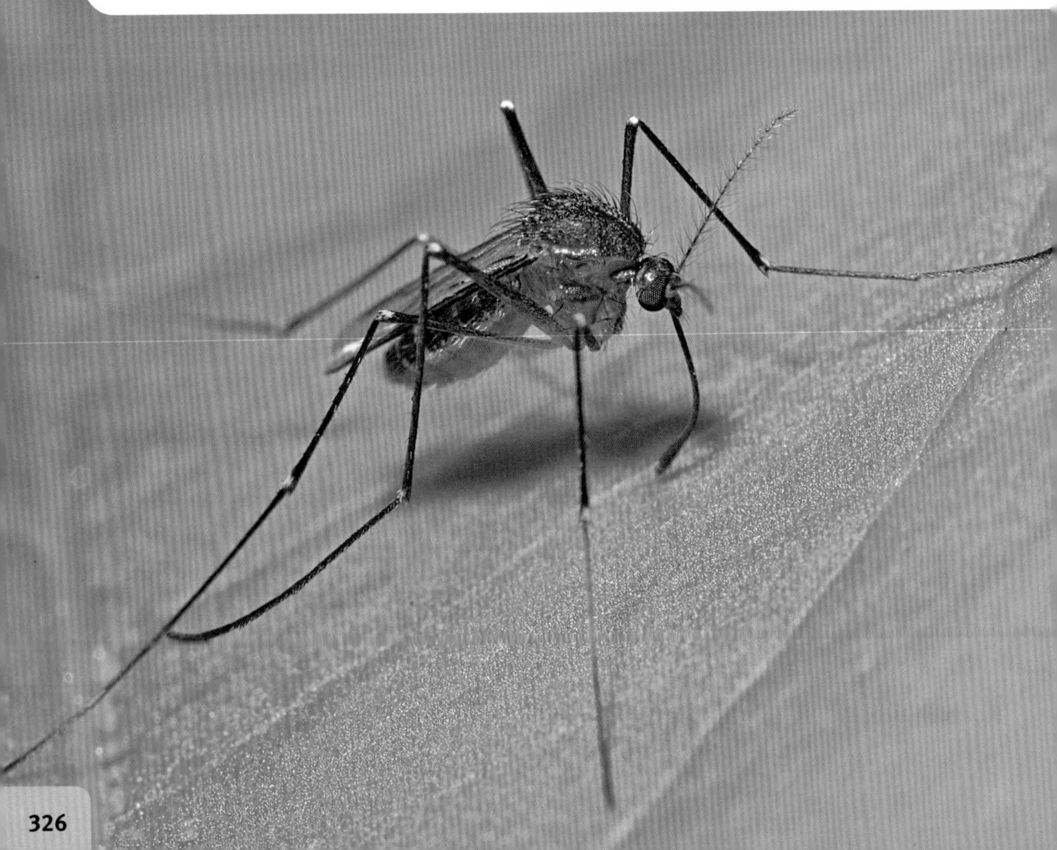

# Biting Midge and Damselfly

Look closely at the wings of this Fragile Forktail damselfly (*Ischnura posita*) to see a minute fly sucking blood out of one of its wing veins. The fly (*Forcipomyia* sp.) belongs to the same family (Ceratopogonidae) as the familiar punkies or no-see-ums that bite you and me on warm summer evenings. The damselfly is a common eastern North American species.

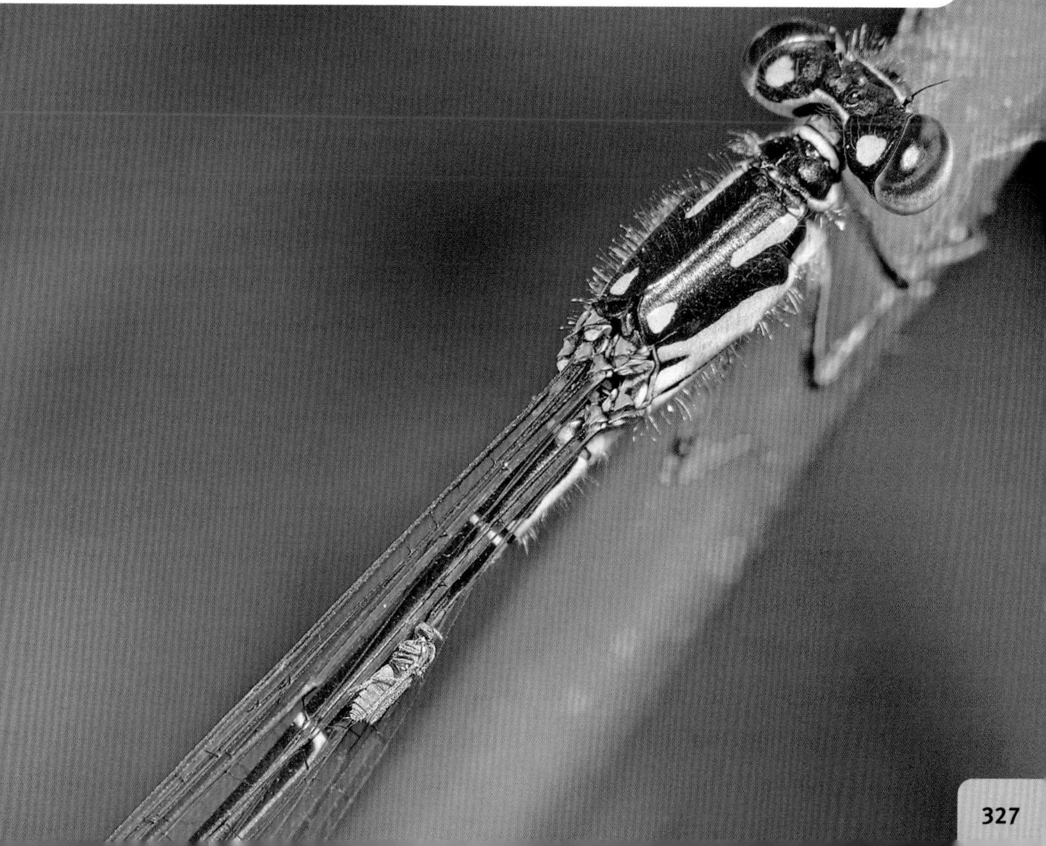

# Meniscus Midge

This odd-looking insect, photographed on the surface of a Chilean stream, is the larva of a dixid midge or meniscus midge (family Dixidae). Like some kinds of mosquito larvae, dixid midge larvae live at the water's surface, where they filter food from the surface film. Unlike mosquitoes, dixid midge larvae often live on flowing waters, although they stay near the shore or the edges of floating vegetation.

# Glowworm

These glistening traps dangling from the moist moss of a New Zealand gully are fishing lines made by a New Zealand glowworm, the larva of a fungus gnat, *Arachnocampa luminosa* (family Keroplatidae). When other small insects get caught in the sticky globules that adorn the lines, the larva will reel in the line and eat the catch. Glowworms attract their prey with an ethereal bluish glow—displays of glowworms in dark caves are famous tourist attractions in New Zealand.

# Lovebug

The male of this aptly named pair of Lovebugs (*Plecia nearctica*, family Bibionidae) is the one with the huge eyes, which are used to spot a female arriving at a swarm of like-minded hovering males. Once a Lovebug male obtains a mate he hangs on to her for a long time; these frequently irritatingly abundant flies are most often seen in copula. Swarms of Lovebugs are a nuisance on highways in the southeastern United States, where their squished bodies make unwelcome hood adornments and can cause paint blemishes.

# Micro Bee Fly

This tiny (about 0.08 inch/2 mm), humpbacked *Mythicomyia* (family Mythicomyiidae) probably developed underground as a parasite on the larva of a solitary bee. Adult *Mythicomyia* such as this male are abundant in dry areas of western North America, often on *Eriogonum* flowers. Mythicomyiidae are closely related to bee flies, and were until recently treated as part of the bee fly family.

# Bee Fly

Not all bee flies (family Bombyliidae) have long beaks, but those that do use them as straws to imbibe nectar from deep in selected flowers. This *Parasystoechus flavescens* is hovering over a purple flower in a garden near Santiago, Chile. Most bee fly larvae are parasitic or predaceous on immature stages of other insects, usually in concealed places such as bee or wasp cells or buried grasshopper egg pods.

# Bee Fly



Most of the 4,500 or so world species of bee flies (family Bombyliidae) occur in relatively arid places, and this *Paranthrax rufiventris* is one of the many species found along the hot, dry coast of central Chile. Most bee fly larvae are parasitoids, while adults feed on nectar and pollen.

# Bee Fly

The five colorful species in the bee fly genus *Hyperalonia* (this is *H. chilensis*) are widespread in South America, where some attack sand-nesting solitary wasps. This female fly is hovering over a sand wasp burrow; she will swiftly dart down to squirt an egg into the nest. The bee fly's larvae will attach itself to the wasp larvae and slowly suck out their body contents.

# Tangle-veined Fly



Tangle-veined flies (family Nemestrinidae) are so called because of the way their wing veins loop and twist. These spectacularly swift fliers are most often seen as they hover in one spot, often over a desert flower. Tangle-veined flies are abundant in Chile; this one, *Trichophthalma subaurata*, was photographed near Santiago. Nothing is known of the biology of this genus, but related genera develop as parasitoids of scarab larvae and nymphal grasshoppers.

# Tangle-veined Fly

This Chilean tangle-veined fly, *Trichophthalma lundbecki*, has its strikingly long proboscis largely hidden deep in a flower. Despite this sort of conspicuous behavior of the bee-sized adult tangle-veined flies, very little is known about the biology of this family (Nemestrinidae). The few species with known life cycles hatch from their eggs as active larvae that hunt out hosts—beetle larvae or young grasshoppers—which they then penetrate and kill as internal parasitoids (parasitoids, unlike parasites, routinely kill their hosts).

# Deer Fly



Deer flies (*Chrysops* spp., family Tabanidae), such as this *Chrysops aberrans* photographed on a concrete bridge wall in Ontario, are stunningly beautiful insects. They would probably be admired and collected for the winged jewels they are if it were not for their propensity for using scissors-like mandibles to slice into your skin for a meal of blood. Only females bite, as is true for most biting flies except for Stable Flies and other biting Muscidae.

# Horse Fly

The brilliantly colored eyes that adorn many living Tabanidae (horse flies, deer flies and relatives) fade in death as the structure that creates the color patterns collapses. The multicolored eyes of this Bolivian *Diachlorus bicinctus* would fade to dull brown in a collection of pinned specimens, as do the brilliantly mottled eyes of deer flies.

# Horse Fly



Male horse flies do not share the propensity of some female horse flies to slice chunks out of vertebrate skin in order to imbibe the underlying blood, and therefore lack the biting mouthparts of the female. They also differ from females in having large eyes that meet above the head, often giving them—like this *Tabanus superjumentarius* from the eastern United States—a big-headed appearance.

# Pangonine Horse Fly

This spectacularly slender-snouted fly, *Mycteromyia conica*, is a horse fly (subfamily Pangoniinae, family Tabanidae) that uses its mouthparts to probe flowers such as this bright orange *Alstroemeria* (inset) rather than flesh. Long-beaked flies are common flower visitors in central Chile; some species are able to bring their long snouts into play to inflict a painful bite.

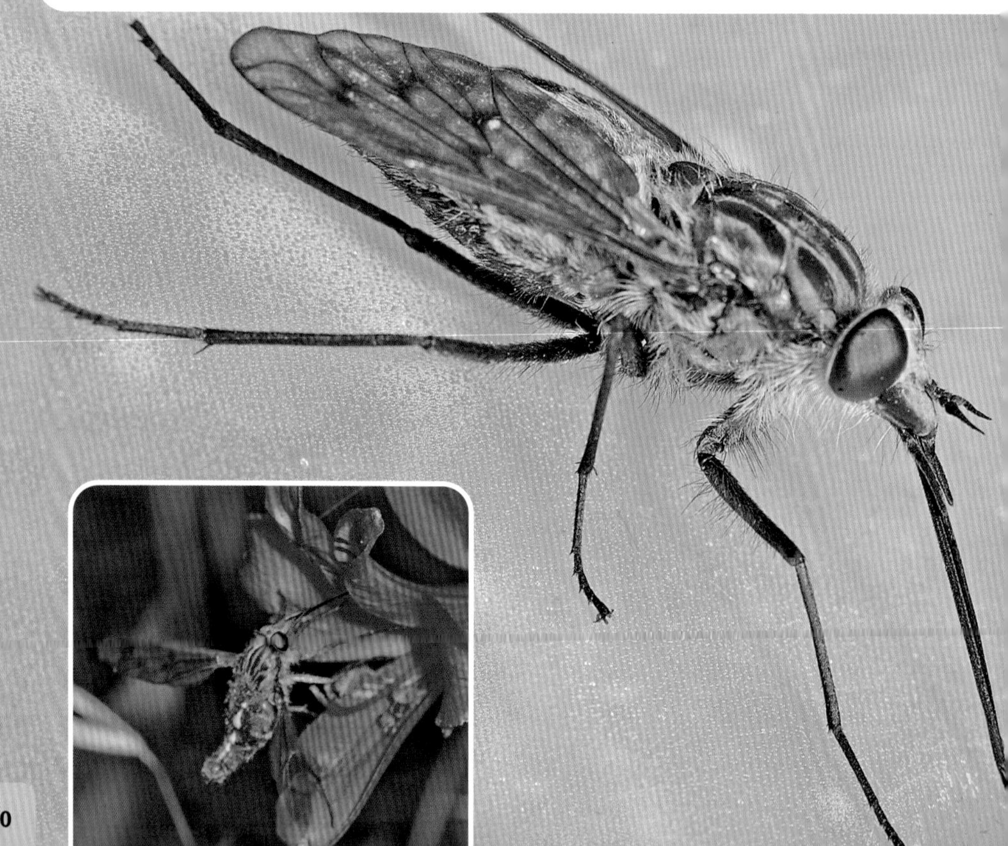

# Pangonine Horse Fly

Long-beaked horse flies in the subfamily Pangoninae are common in south temperate countries but relatively uncommon in North America. The few North American species in this subfamily are mostly western, like this *Esenbeckia delta* taking nectar from an Arizona flower.

# Small-headed Fly

Small-headed flies (family Acroceridae) are parasitoids that develop inside spiders, and the adults are presumably small-headed because they are able leave the job of seeking a spider host to their enormous broods. Their thousands of tiny eggs hatch into active larvae that hunt down a spider host, burrow inside, and then transform into a killer parasitoid, often delaying development until the host spider is big enough to make a decent meal. This humpbacked species perched on the edge of a Chilean flower is a *Megalybus*.

# Soldier Fly

Soldier flies (family Stratiomyidae) are especially diverse in tropical regions, where they are associated with a range of habitats. This brightly colored *Heptozus* from Costa Rica is an undescribed species that probably breeds in pockets of decomposing material between leaves of living cloud-forest plants.

# Soldier Fly

Soldier flies (family Stratiomyidae) are harmless insects, but they often look very much like bees or wasps. Many North American soldier flies are close mimics of bees, but this Bolivian *Chrysochlorina* species resembles a paper wasp (*Angiopolybia* sp., inset), here seen feeding on honeydew almost alongside its dipteran doppelganger.

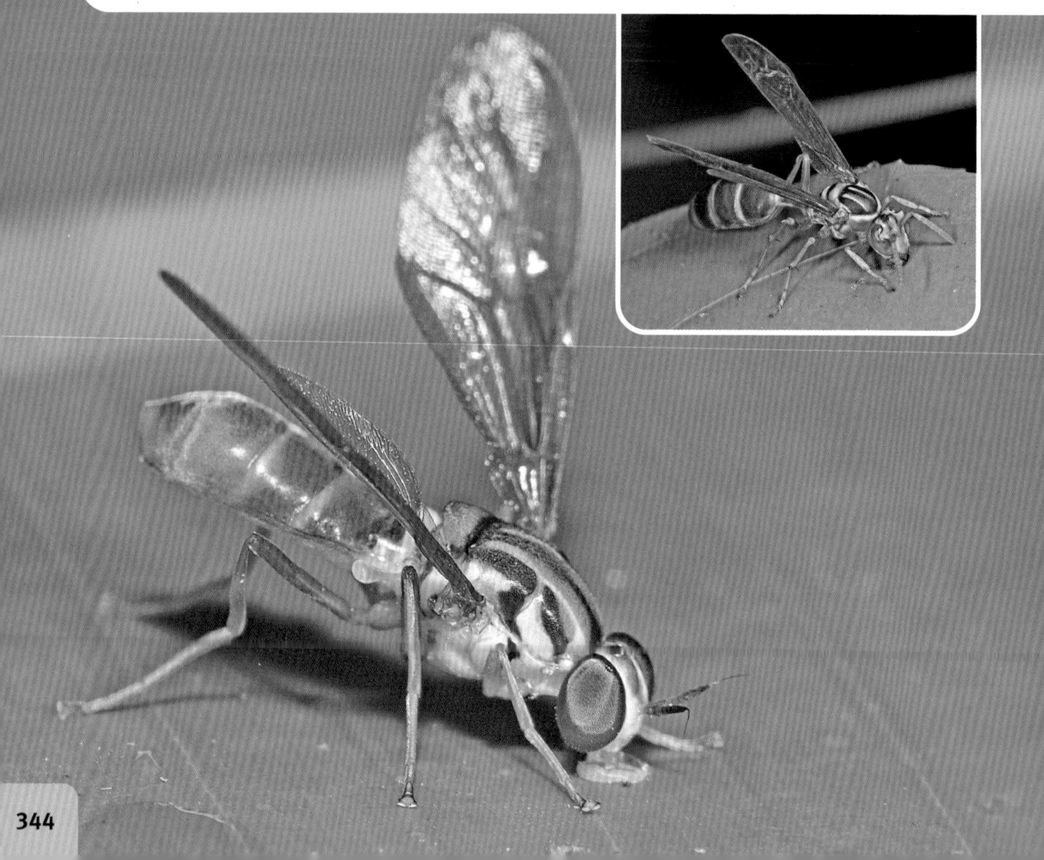

# Soldier Fly

This soldier fly (*Hermetia comstocki*, family Stratiomyidae) is part of a complex of similarly colored wasps and flies that includes brightly colored stinging wasps honestly advertising their defenses with bright colors, as well as harmless fly mimics such as this soldier fly and some flower flies (see page 386).

# Soldier Fly

The brightly colored soldier flies (family Stratiomyidae) in the genus *Caloparyphus*, such as this *C. decemmaculatus* from New Mexico, occur in shallow water, where the flattened, tough-skinned larvae usually sprawl on the submerged leaves of aquatic plants. Most species are found in still water, but some are found in seeps (thin films of flowing water).

# Soldier Fly

The 2,000 or so world species of soldier flies (family Stratiomyidae) are impressively diverse in size, shape and color. Most, like this orange Costa Rican *Merosargus*, are relatively slow-moving flies that normally overlap their wings flat across their backs. Larvae of several species of *Merosargus* develop in the bracts and flowers of *Heliconia* (false bird-of-paradise) plants.

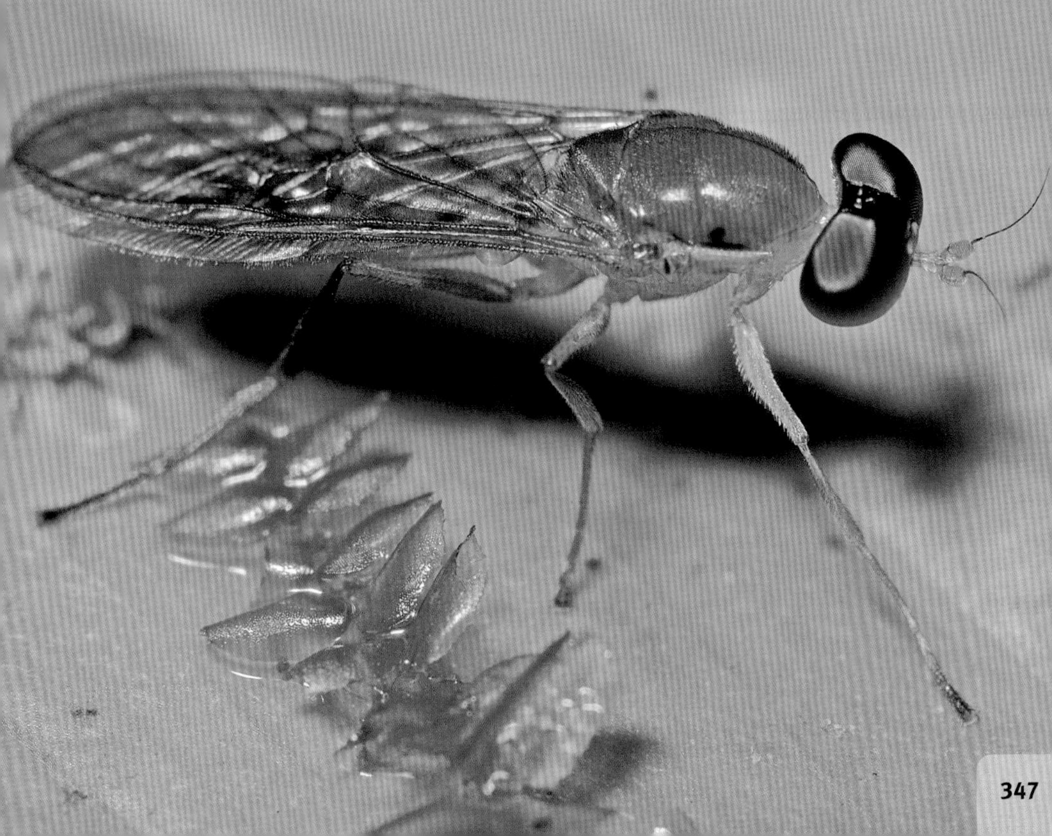

# Soldier Fly

Soldier flies (family Stratiomyiidae) develop in a variety of aquatic and terrestrial habitats, including decomposing vegetation. These mating *Ptecticus* were photographed in the rainforest of Bolivia, but similar members of the same genus can be found around compost heaps in North America.

# Wingless Soldier Fly



The soldier fly family (Stratiomyidae) is diverse, with more than 2,000 species divided into several subfamilies. This Tasmanian wingless soldier fly, *Boreoides tasmaniensis*, is an unusual member of the subfamily Chiromyzinae, and this West Australian species (inset) is a more typical soldier fly in the subfamily Stratiomyiinae.

# Giant Wood-boring Fly

Pantophthalmidae are the among the largest of all flies, sometimes attaining lengths of more than 2 inches (5 cm). Despite their formidable horse fly–like appearance, these hefty insects don't bite—in fact they don't even feed during their short adult lives. Larvae develop as wood borers in dead or dying trees throughout the neotropics. This *Pantophthalmus* was photographed in Bolivia.

# Snipe Fly

The compound eyes of insects are made up of many individual simple eyes, or ommatidia. Males of many insects such as this snipe fly (*Chrysopilus* sp., family Rhagionidae) have relatively large eyes, with the ommatidia of the top half especially well developed. This was one of many elusive individuals perched on the trunk of a tree in Cuba.

# Long-legged Fly

Long-legged flies (family Dolichopodidae), such as this brilliantly green-eyed *Neurigona* on an Ontario garden plant, are predators that use their spiky lower lips to capture small prey. *Neurigona* species are often seen on tree trunks, where they feed on small, soft-bodied arthropods like springtails, scales and mites.

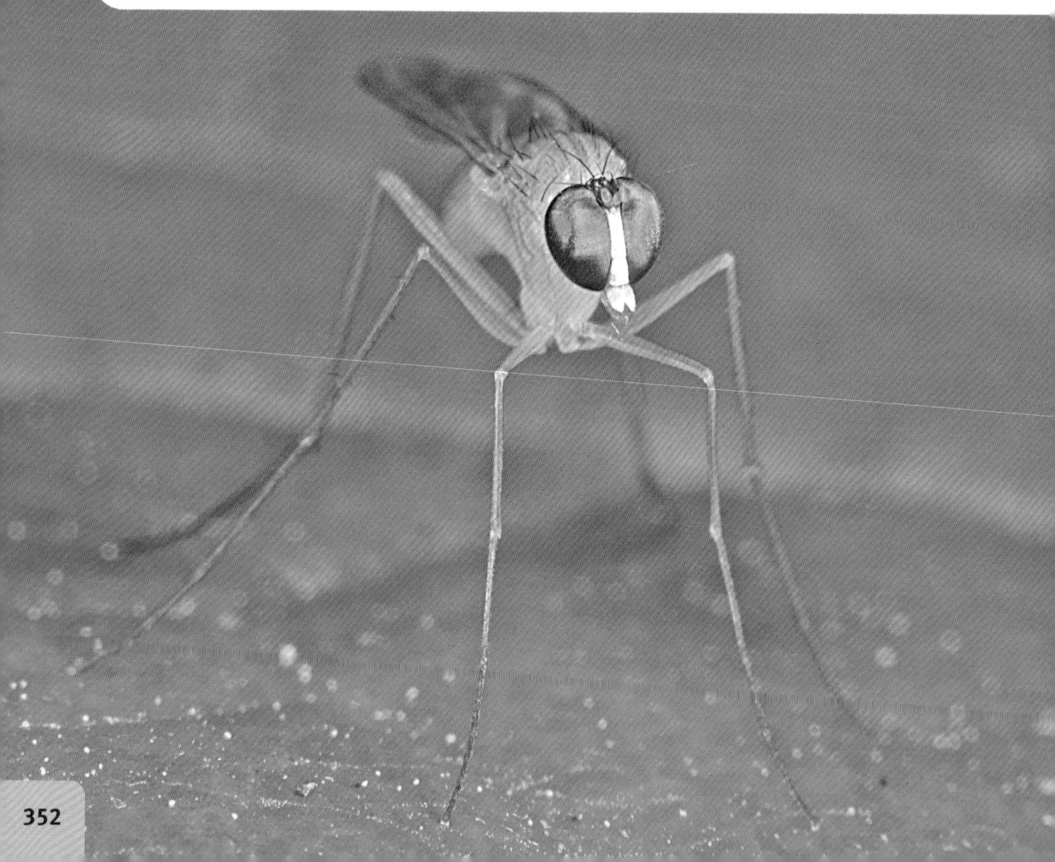

# Long-legged Fly

Brilliantly metallic flies in the genus *Condostylus* are among the most common terrestrial long-legged flies (family Dolichopodidae); they can be seen hunting small insects on foliage almost anywhere. This *Condylostylus caesar* is perched on a leaf overhanging a Bolivian rainforest trail.

# Long-legged Fly

Male long-legged flies in the genus *Dolichopus* (family Dolichopodidae) often have elaborate ornaments that are used in courting. Males of this Canadian species have little black-and-white flags at the ends of their front legs; they are waved in front of females to attract their attention, but it looks like one of these males is waving in vain.

# Long-legged Fly

Aquatic insects are especially vulnerable as they transform from the underwater immature stages to the aerial winged stages, and busy emergence sites such as streamside rocks are often lined with predaceous dance flies and long-legged flies. This long-legged fly (family Dolichopodidae) has just used the broad, spiky lobes of its lower lip to nail a mayfly subimago emerging from a northern Ontario river.

# Long-legged Fly

This species of long-legged fly (*Thambemyia borealis*, family Dolichopodidae) is now common on the rocks of the Peruvian coast, including the city of Lima, where this photo was taken. This western Pacific species was probably accidentally introduced to the Pacific coast of South America from Japan. It preys on small insects along the rocky coast.

# Long-legged Fly

Most long-legged flies (Dolichopodidae) mash up soft-bodied prey using mouthparts that include armed lobes on a broad lower lip (labium), generating and sucking up a juicy pulp. This *Dolichopus* is sucking up a writhing oligochaete worm along the edge of an Arizona stream.

# Dance Fly

This dance fly (*Chelipoda* sp., family Empididae) belongs to a subfamily (Hemerodromiinae) usually associated with aquatic environments. This pair is mating on seashore rocks in Lima, Peru, but members of the same genus are found along freshwater and marine shorelines north to Canada.

# Dance Fly

All dance flies (family Empididae) are predators, and many have one or more pairs of legs modified to grab other insects. This small Costa Rican dance fly (*Chelifera* sp.) has pincer-like forelegs that it is using to hang on to a minute midge (family Chironomidae). *Chelifera* is a widespread genus, and similar flies can be found throughout North America.

# Dance Fly

The little pots of sugary fluids produced by some plants such as this Bolivian *Inga* are called extrafloral nectaries, and they usually function to attract ants that in turn protect the leaves from predation. Extrafloral nectaries, however, attract a variety of insects such as this dance fly (*Macrostomus* sp., family Empididae).

# Dance Fly

Females of many dance flies (family Empididae) are predators but do not hunt for themselves, instead relying on prey brought to them by suitors bearing "nuptial gifts." This male *Rhamphomyia longicauda* has captured a caddisfly and will fly with it into a swarm of females, his nuptial gift giving him an opportunity to choose the most fecund-looking female in the swarm. Females of this species are ornamented to look as big as possible, and they enhance their fecund appearance by puffing out their abdomens like little balloons when they swarm. This is a common eastern North American species that swarms in late summer evenings.

# Dance Fly

A few insects are remarkably heat-tolerant, and some even use smoke as a cue to fly into still-smoldering fires, which they use as a new source of food for their larvae (some wood-boring beetles, for example) or a hot place for mating. These dance flies (family Empididae), which were among many that landed and mated on the sizzling hot surfaces around a smoky campfire in Ontario, belong to a genus (*Hormopeza*) well-known for the latter behavior. Dance flies are predators, and *Hormpopeza* often feed on other flies attracted to smoke, including smoke flies (*Microsania* spp., family Platypezidae).

# Dance Fly

This elongate dance fly from Ecuador (*Aplomera* sp., family Empididae) has used its stout hind legs to grab a metallic green long-legged fly (family Dolichopodidae). The stout beak sticking straight down from the dance fly's head is used to impale its prey.

# Dance Fly

Dance flies (family Empididae) such as this Chilean *Empis fulvicollis* are common visitors to flowers. The long beak of this and other dance flies is not just used for nectar feeding as is the proboscis of related bee flies. Dance flies are predators that impale other insects, consuming their contents.

# Atelestid and Brachystomatid Flies

These two long-beaked flies visiting white flowers are south temperate species in families closely related to the dance fly family, Empididae. This black and brown fly (inset) visiting a yellow-centered flower in New Zealand is in the austral genus *Ceratomerus* (family Brachystomatidae). *Ceratomerus* occurs in New Zealand and Australia in the same water-splashed habitats where you would find certain dance flies in the northern hemisphere, much the way that marsupials such as kangaroos occupy niches that would be filled by familiar mammals in the northern hemisphere. This shining black fly straddling four of the ten petals of a white flower belongs to the Chilean genus *Acarteroptera* in the enigmatic family Atelestidae.

# Robber Fly

Although this Canadian *Laphria sicula* doesn't seem to need much protection in order to attack and eat a small midge (family Chironomidae), all robber flies (family Asilidae) have a protective tuft of bristles, called a mystax, separating their face from potentially struggling victims.

# Robber Fly

This Bolivian robber fly (*Lampria clavipes*, family Asilidae) has just impaled a small parasitic wasp and is imbibing its liquefied contents through a blade-like beak. Robber flies subdue their prey and dissolve their victim's body contents with an injection of neurotoxic and proteolytic saliva.

# Robber Fly

Robber flies (family Asilidae) in the genus *Lampria*, such as this *L. dives* from Bolivia, are closely related to the larger and more common bee-like robber flies (*Laphria* spp.). Like all robber flies they have widely separated eyes and a tuft of long hairs above a prominent beak, but *Lampria* and *Laphria* have unusually flat, blade-like beaks.

# Robber Fly

Robber flies in the genus *Laphria* have a flat, knife-like beak that is often used to slip between the hard protective wing covers of beetle prey. Many members of this genus are stunning mimics of bumblebees, but this American coastal plain species, *Laphria saffrana*, is a dead ringer for a common vespid wasp, the Southern Yellowjacket.

# Robber Fly

Although this *Diogmites* robber fly (family Asilidae) is from Bolivia, members of the genus *Diogmites* look pretty much the same from Canada to Argentina. They also behave much the same, characteristically hanging from vegetation by their long front legs while imbibing the contents of insect prey held by the middle and hind legs. The damselfly that is the main course here has a parasitic wasp attached to the tip of its abdomen; it seems to have been caught in the act of trying to dislodge it.

# Robber Fly

This robber fly (family Asilidae) is feeding on a small midge in a remote Arizona canyon, one of the few places where this rare, Arizona-only robber fly, *Ommatius bromleyi*, occurs.

# Robber Fly

The small robber flies in the genus *Holcocephala* often feed on tiny midges and springtails, although this Bolivian fly has impaled a minute beetle. *Holcocephala* is a widespread genus, with similar species in both temperate and tropical regions.

# Robber Fly



The large robber flies in the genus *Proctacanthus* are often seen tackling big insects such as bumble bees, wasps and even dragonflies. This *Proctacanthus nearno*, a southwestern American species, has just nailed a skipper butterfly, impaling it through the top of its thorax.

# Robber Fly

This robber fly (family Asilidae) has impaled a bee fly (family Bombyliidae) through the back of the thorax. Although here photographed in New Mexico, this species of robber fly, *Stichopogon trifasciatus*, is common along gravelly lake or river margins from South America to Canada.

# Robber Fly

This Chilean robber fly (*Scylaticus lugens*) has impaled a beetle through the side of its body. Several robber flies (family Asilidae) specialize in hunting beetles, almost invariably nailing them in flight, when their hard wing covers are spread and the body is relatively unprotected.

# Robber Fly

This Chilean robber fly, *Hexameritia micans*, was one of several similar flies searching for jumping plant lice (family Psyllidae) on a little patch of vegetation on a coastal sand dune. The fly's beak is penetrating its tiny green prey right behind the head.

# Robber Fly



The brilliant blue-green eyes of robber flies in the genus *Megophorus* render them among the most attractive of flies. *Megophorus* species, which look and behave much like the small leafcutter bees that are among their usual prey, have a remarkable habit of laying eggs in case-like masses on twigs; upon hatching, larvae drop to the ground to become subterranean predators. This one is scanning for prey from the end of a twig in a New Mexico desert.

# Robber Fly

Members of the large and widespread robber fly genus *Mallophora* (family Asilidae), such as this *Mallophora fautrix* eating a honey bee in New Mexico, are aptly known as bee-killers. They are often attended by small kleptoparasitic flies (family Milichiidae) that lap up the juices leaking from stinging prey impaled and liquefied for consumption by these large robber flies.

# Robber Fly

This enormous robber fly, *Wyleia mydas*, is an uncommon southwestern American species that looks and behaves exactly like tarantula hawks (*Pepsis* spp., family Pompilidae), which occur in the same places. Since tarantula hawks have one of the biggest stings of all wasps, predators wisely steer clear of both the wasps and the similar flies. The fly's species name refers to a similarity between these big black robber flies and some species of mydas flies (family Mydidae), which also mimic tarantula hawks (page 489).

# Mydas Fly

Mydas flies (family Mydidae) look a bit like their fiercely predaceous relatives the robber flies, although they lack the blade-like mouthparts used by robber flies to impale their victims; instead they sometimes have elongate mouthparts used to imbibe nectar. The long-beaked species are mostly associated with flowers in areas with relatively hot, dry climates, and include the endangered Delhi Sands Flower-loving Fly, *Rhaphiomidas terminatus*, of California as well as this Chilean species, *Mitrodetus dentitarsus*.

# Mydas Fly

Most mydas flies (family Mydidae) live in arid areas, and these are among the many species found in the American southwest. This brown fly is a relatively small (about half an inch) *Opomydas* species and the black and red fly (inset) is a large (over an inch) *Mydas* species, one of several similar species that mimic tarantula hawks (spider wasps in the genus *Pepsis*). This harmless fly's orange back resembles the warning color on the wings of conspicuously well-armed *Pepsis* wasps that abound throughout the southwest (page 489).

# Stiletto Fly

Stiletto flies (family Therevidae), such as this North American *Acrosathe vialis*, look a bit like robber flies but lack the biting mouthparts and protective facial hair of their predaceous relatives. Although unfamiliar to most naturalists, this group includes more than 1,500 species worldwide, mostly from arid areas, where their larvae are major subterranean predators.

# Flower Fly

Pollen feeding is well known amongst Syrphidae (flower flies), and this *Chalcosyrphus* is clearly one of those species able to ingest pollen grains. *Chalcosyrphus pigra* is a widespread species, ranging from eastern Canada to California.

# Flower Fly

Flower flies (family Syrphidae) are often called hover flies for their familiar habit of hovering in one spot, usually as single individuals but even occasionally in tandem, as demonstrated by these flying united *Toxomerus*. These were photographed in Costa Rica, but similar *Toxomerus* species are common in gardens over much of the world.

# Flower Fly



Flower flies, such as this *Meromacrus acutus* nectaring on a South Carolina flower, often look and behave like bees or wasps, presumably causing potential predators to think twice before attacking. *Meromacrus* species, like similar species of *Milesia* and several other flower fly genera, look and act remarkably like yellowjacket wasps and hornets.

# Flower Fly

Members of the genus *Spilomyia* are among the most impressive wasp mimics in the family Syrphidae (flower flies), often resembling co-occuring potter wasps and social wasps (family Vespidae) in size, shape and movement. This southwestern American species, *Spilomyia kahli*, is probably a mimic of similarly brightly colored southwestern potter wasps such as this *Euodynerus provisoreus* (inset).

# Flower Fly



The tiny flower flies in the genus *Orthonevra* have amazing eyes decorated with intricate patterns such as the squiggly brown lines on the eyes of this *Orthonevra nitida*.

# Flower Fly

This gaudily metallic Australian flower fly belongs to the genus *Australis*, an oriental-Australian genus of Syrphidae described in 2003 by syrphid expert F. Christian Thompson. Although the genus is new, the species, *A. pulchella*, was discovered and named (as part of the large genus *Eristalis*) 157 years earlier. Like other species related to *Eristalis*, this species probably has aquatic larvae that might be considered rat-tailed maggots because they breathe through a long, retractile siphon that looks like a rat's tail.

# Flower Fly

This *Copestylum trifasciata* (family Syrphidae) was one of many flies seeking moisture along the bed of an Arizona stream. Its constantly moving antennae look a bit strange because the arista, a normally thin and hairlike antennal structure, is broad and feathery, giving the whole antenna a two-pronged appearance.

# Mexican Cactus Fly

The largest insect visiting this Arizona flower is a Mexican Cactus Fly, *Copestylum mexicana*, a flower fly (family Syrphidae) common in not only Mexico but also the American southwest. Adults are found on flowers, but larvae of this and many related species develop in rotting cactus stems.

# Flower Fly

The flower fly genus *Copestylum* is the largest genus of flower flies in the world, with well over 300 named species and at least another hundred species recognized by specialists but not yet named. Most species occur in Central and South America, but the genus ranges north to Canada. This *C. sexmaculatum* was photographed in South Carolina. Larval *Copestylum*, which breathe through back spiracles on the end of a long tube, are characteristic of wet plant material with lots of bacteria, such as decaying cacti.

# Flower Fly

Many flower flies (family Syrphidae) have long mouthparts used to feed in flowers, and the front of the head is often elongated to sheath the long mouthparts when they are not in use. That gives members of some groups, such as the widespread genus *Rhingia*—this North American *R. nasica* is hanging under a raspberry flower—their characteristic long snouts.

# Flower Fly

Flower flies in the genus *Chrysotoxum*, like this one feeding at a Scarlet Cinquefoil (*Potentilla thurberi*) flower in New Mexico, are convincing mimics of yellowjacket wasps such as this *Vespula pennsylvanica* (inset) photographed on the same plant. The two insects are almost impossible to distinguish while in flight and are similar enough even standing still that most birds would think twice about tackling the defenseless fly.

# Flower Fly

Flower flies in the small subfamily Microdontinae are unusual insects that are invariably associated with ant nests. The remarkably mollusk-like larvae are myrmecophiles that develop inside the nests, probably eating ant larvae. Adults are often mimics of bees, sometimes even having fake pollen baskets on their hind legs. This larval *Microdon* (inset) is from a Canadian carpenter ant nest; this small orange adult on a leaf-bound ant nest is from Ecuador.

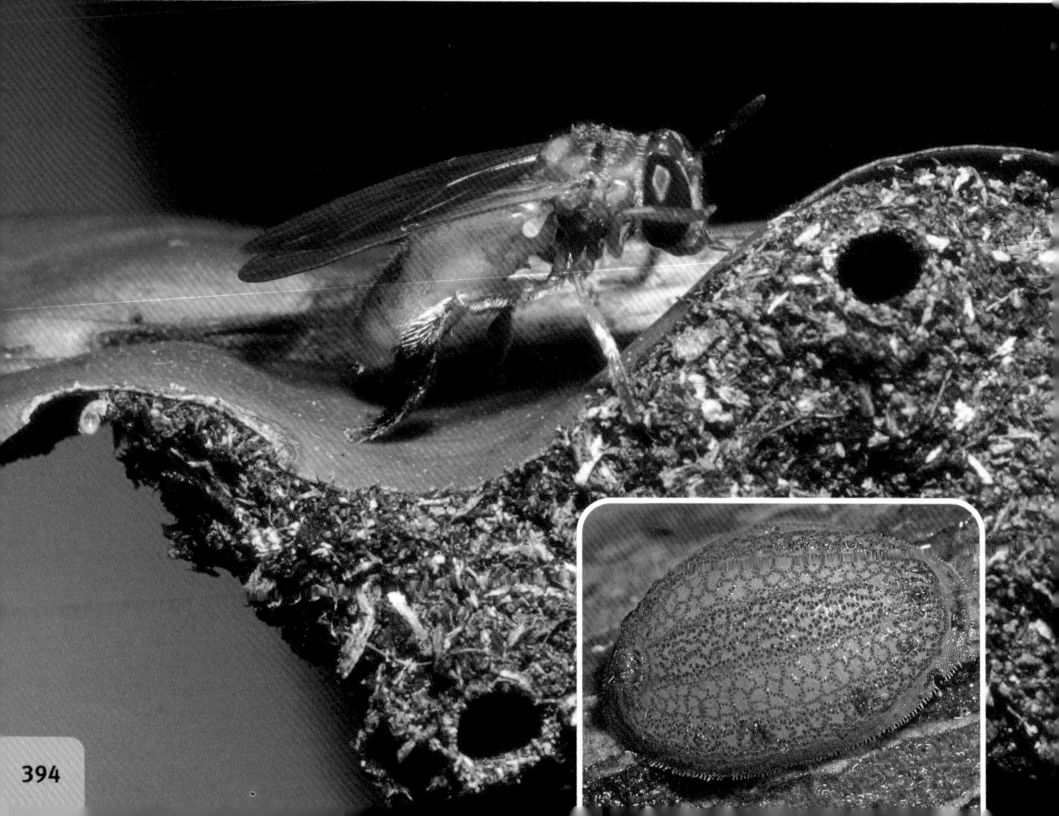

# Big-headed Fly

Big-headed flies (family Pipunculidae), such as this *Eudorylas* touching down on a leaf in eastern Canada, are parasitoids that often hover stock-still over bits of meadow or foliage before spotting a host and swooping down to attack. Eggs are injected into the host, usually a leafhopper, where they hatch into larvae that consume the hapless hopper from inside.

# Thick-headed Fly

Thick-headed flies (family Conopidae) in *Physocephala* and related genera are sometimes called bee-bombers because the females dive-bomb adult bees and wasps, gripping them with the aid of a prominent abdominal knob long enough to inject them with eggs. The fly larvae develop inside the bees, ultimately killing them. North American bumble bees are sometimes heavily parasitized by *Physocephala* species, as are some crabronid waps. This North American species is *Physocephala clavata*.

# Fruit Fly

Many members of the true fruit fly family (Tephritidae) induce plants to make custom domiciles called galls. The species shown here, *Rachiptera limbata*, is responsible for conspicuous white galls that look like bumpy marshmallows on the twigs of the common Chilean shrub *Baccharis linearis*. Despite their soft and bubbly appearance, these galls are surprisingly solid. The galls are abundant and conspicuous, but the adult fly that induces them by laying eggs in the twigs is short-lived and rarely seen.

# Fruit Fly

Members of the family Tephritidae, usually called fruit flies because of the unwelcome habits of some serious agricultural pests in the family, are often colorful flies with bold wing markings. Not all develop in fruits; many feed on roots, stems, leaves, galls and even (rarely) other insects. Fruit flies occur throughout the world, but the fly shown here—a *Pseudophorellia acrostichalis* from Bolivia—is a little little-known species that lives high in the Andes.

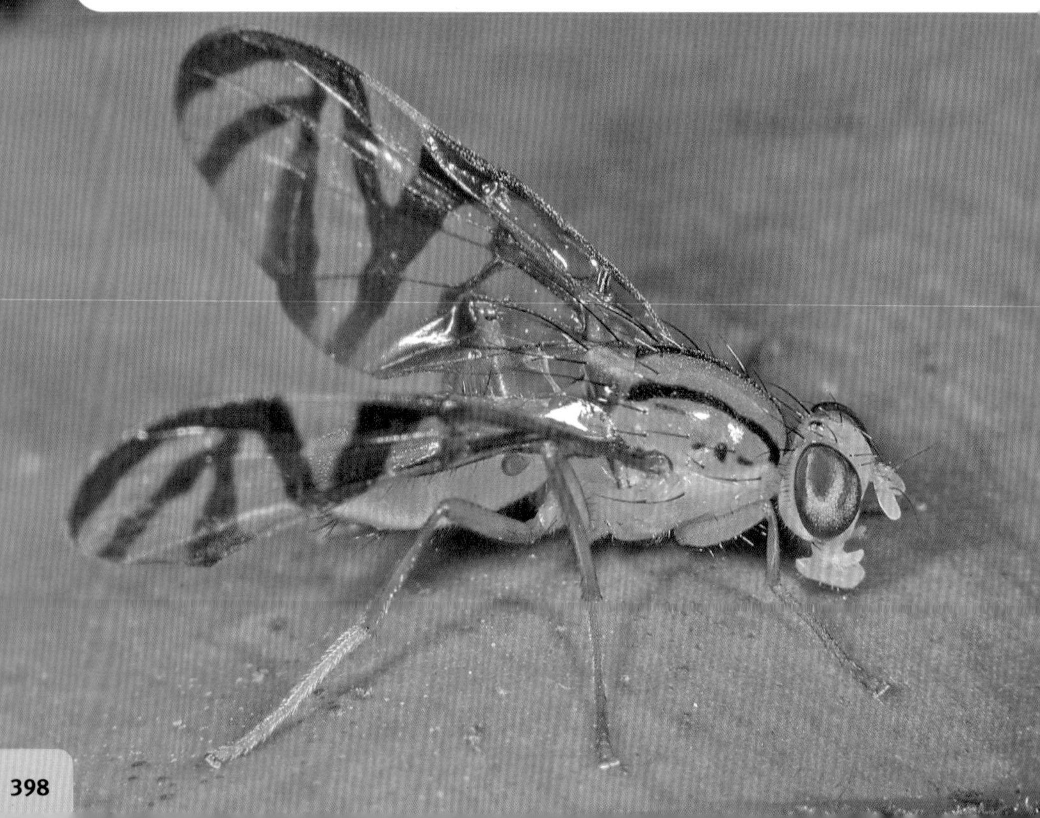

# Picture-winged Fly

Opuntia cacti such as this one in New Mexico provide a spine-protected home for a wide variety of specialized bugs, beetles and flies, including a couple of species of picture-winged flies (family Ulidiidae, also known as Otitidae). The most distinctive of these is *Stictomyia longicornis*, one of several species of acalyptrate flies that have a habit of folding the wings tight against the body so they look more like beetles than flies.

# Picture-winged Fly

Flies in several families have developed widened heads, usually associated with male–male jousting for prime mating territories, but few take their head-stretching to the extreme of this male *Plagiocephalus latifrons* (family Ulidiidae), photographed in Bolivia. Only the males of this widespread neotropical species have widened heads.

# Richardiid Fly



Males of many flies in several different families have elaborate structures that look and function like the antlers of deer or elk. The antler-like cheek processes of this male *Richardia* (family Richardiidae) probably serve in ritual battles over mating territories, with the best-endowed male hanging on to the turf.

# Richardiid Fly

Although many insects have special appendages, called ovipositors, for laying eggs, flies (order Diptera) have lost their ovipositors and have to use the whole tip of the abdomen to deliver their eggs. The stiff tip of the abdomen of this *Beebeomyia* (family Richardiidae) is like a tapered telescope that can be extended to stick eggs between the layers of a bud on a Costa Rican bromeliad flower.

# Richardiid Fly

The two flies sharing this bit of organic material are a relatively slender *Grallipeza* (family Micropezidae) and a broader, paler *Coilomelopia* (family Richardiidae), which characteristically feeds with its rear-end pointed up, looking much like the head of a potentially aggressive black-eyed insect.

# Clusiid Fly

Small flies in the family Clusiidae are rarely noticed, but they seem to come out of the woodwork when presented with the right attractants. This *Sobarocephala rubsaamenii*, attracted to a bird dropping in Bolivia, is one of hundreds of species of the genus *Sobarocephala* in South America, most of which remain undescribed (that is, new to science).

# Clusiid Fly



Flies in the family Clusiidae often have elaborate mating behavior, sometimes involving mating sites (leks) where males aggregate and joust for position while waiting for females to arrive. When this female *Sobarocephala latifrons* arrived at a mating site in southern Ontario, she was mobbed by smaller males, including the two you see attending to her here.

# Clusiid Fly

Clusiidae are common flies on fallen logs and similar prominent "arenas" in the forests where males display and compete with one another for mating territories. These broad-headed Australian *Hendelia armiger* start out their interactions by measuring the width of their opponent's head; if they are equally matched they lock spring-like cheek bristles and have a pushing fight, as seen here.

# Odiniid Fly

These *Traginops irrorata* (family Odiniidae) seem to be fighting over a bit of territory on a bleeding oak wound in southern Ontario. One has exposed the complicated bits and pieces of male genitalia, which invariably differ from species to species in most sexually reproducing insects and are often used by insect specialists to distinguish between closely related species.

# Platystomatid Fly

Many flies "kiss" as part of their mating ritual. This Australian platystomatid (*Lenophila* sp., family Platystomatidae) has a particularly elaborate ritual, starting with a "kiss" and followed by the male doing a back-flip over his mate. This species breeds in Western Australian grass trees (Xanthorrhoeaceae).

# Coconut Fly

The Coconut Fly (*Scholastes bimaculatus*, family Platystomatidae) is a common fly on many South Pacific islands, where it breeds in decomposing coconuts. This one was photographed in Hawaii, where the species appears to have been accidentally introduced.

# Antlike Scavenger Fly

Antlike scavenger flies (family Sepsidae) often aggregate in large numbers near the decomposing material in which their larvae develop. These were among thousands of flies on some foliage over a fresh meadow muffin along the edge of a Cuban cattle pasture.

# Kleptoparasitic Fly



This Cuban lynx spider has captured a honeybee and started to imbibe its contents, releasing an aroma of digestive juices and honeybee fluids that is irresistible to dozens of kleptoparasitic flies (*Desmometopa* sp.) in the family Milichiidae. Other kinds of kleptoparasites are attracted to other kinds of chemically protected prey; had this spider captured a stinkbug, its tiny dinner guests would probably have been flies from the family Chloropidae.

# Chloropid Fly

This small fly (*Thaumatomyia* sp., family Chloropidae) was attracted to an injured leaf beetle; it followed the beetle around and spent long periods apparently feeding on exudates on its body. Little is known about the biology of the 42 world species of *Thaumatomyia*, but larvae of known species eat aphids, and adults of some species periodically appear in massive swarms.

# Lauxaniid Fly

The Lauxaniidae is one of the most diverse families of acalyptrate flies—the Acalyptratae is the subgroup of flies that includes fruit flies—and the adults seem to appear in every color and form. This robust striped fly is a *Neodeceia* from Cuba, and the little orange fly (inset) among the false nectaries of a white grass of Parnassus flower is a *Sapromyza* from Canada.

# Shore Fly

Shore flies (family Ephydridae) often have a characteristically bulgy face that usually conceals a big, mop-like labellum used to lap up algae. *Setacera atrovirens* is a common fly on algal mats across North America. The surfaces of still waters are like gigantic traps for windborne pollen, dead or drowning insects and other organic material harvested by a variety of water-walking insects such as this Costa Rican shore fly (*Brachydeutera* sp., inset). Shore flies, as the name suggests, usually live in moist places, where most species feed on algae.

# Shore Fly

Most members of the shore fly family (Ephydridae) eat algae, and many species abound along the moist margins of lakes and ponds. Members of the genus *Ochthera*, however, are predators that eat other insects such as midges and mayflies. This Cuban *Ochtera loreta* has flexed its raptorial forelegs to turn a smaller fly (family Chloropidae) into its next meal.

# Drosophilid Fly

Flies in many families get together in special mating arenas where males go to great lengths to impress females and fight other males for the best bits of territory. Most members of the huge neotropical genus *Zygothrica* (family Drosophilidae) breed in flowers, but almost all aggregate for mating on the surfaces of some kinds of fungi. There they indulge in a variety of elaborate behaviors described by *Zygothrica* expert David Grimaldi as "semaphoring, swaying, flicking, scissoring, vibrating, slashing, jousting, butting, pawing, side-swerving" and more. This pair on a Costa Rican fungus seems to be demonstrating flipping.

# Drosophilid Fly



Although the acalyptrate family Drosophilidae is best known for the laboratory fruit fly, *Drosophila melanogaster*, it is an enormous family that includes parasitoids, parasites and predators of other invertebrates. Most species feed on yeasts and other microorganisms, often in flowers or decaying fruit; the most common species belong to the enormous genera *Drosophila*, *Scaptomyza* and *Leucophenga*. Drosophilids occur throughout the world—this photo shows a Cuban *Leucophenga* with a brilliantly white abdomen.

# Somatiid Fly

The fly family Somatiidae is a small neotropical group with only one genus, *Somatia*. Nothing—other than what you can infer from this photograph of a *Somatia schildi* on a dead caterpillar—is known about the biology of this family. Larvae are unknown.

# Cactus Fly

This cactus fly male (*Glyphidops flavifrons*, family Neriidae) is literally standing guard over his mate as she lays eggs in a damaged cactus stem, protecting her from competing males. The eggs will hatch into larvae that develop in decomposing cactus tissue. Related species live in dead or damaged wood.

# Micropezid Fly

Many insects pretend to be ants in order to deter potential predators, but flies in the family Micropezidae are among the best ant mimics. These images show a short-winged Chilean species, *Cryogonus formicarius* (inset), and a distantly related entirely wingless Australian species, *Badisis ambulans*. Adults of *Badisis ambulans* jump like the local ants they resemble; larvae develop only within the pitchers of the rare and endangered Albany Pitcher Plant, *Cephalotus follicularis*, an insectivorous plant found only in a small area in Western Australia. Larvae of *Cryogonus* are unknown, but related species live in the root nodules of legumes.

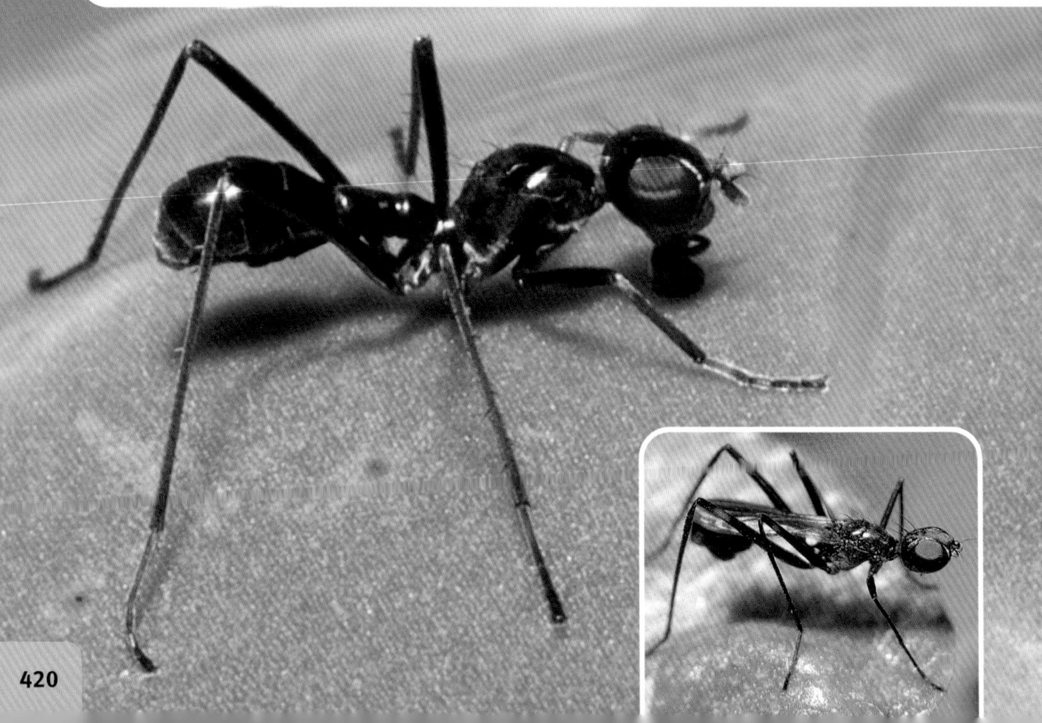

# Micropezid Fly



Micropezid flies often wave the white tips of their front legs much the same way as similar wasps wave their antennae. This orange male *Grallipeza placida*, from Cuba, seems to be dancing to attract a mate, and he has even puffed out what are probably "perfume pouches"—thin-walled swollen areas near the base of its abdomen. The more brightly colored individual is a female of an unnamed species in an undescribed genus. Not much is known about micropezid larvae, but most develop in decaying material.

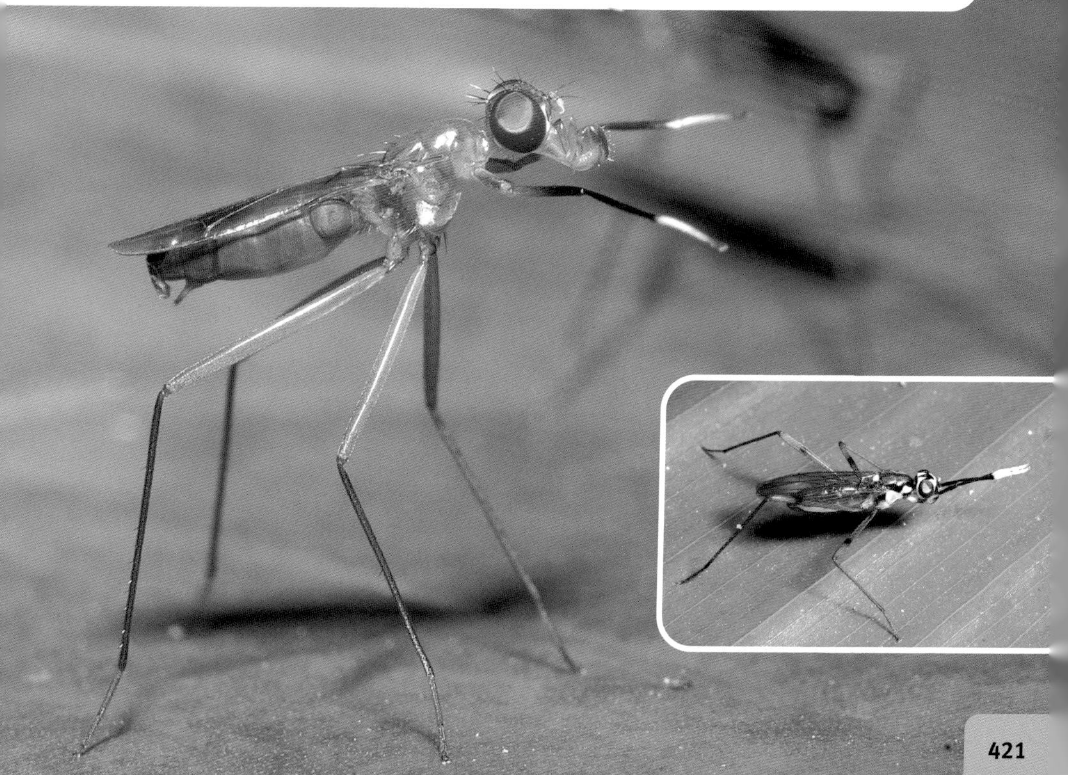

# Micropezid Fly

Like many micropezid flies (family Micropezidae), members of the large neotropical genus *Scipopus* have a habit of locking lips as part of an elaborate courtship ritual. Some evidence suggests that this is more of an oral exchange than a kiss, since the male seems to be transferring nutritious fluids to his mate.

# Stalk-eyed Fly



Stalk-eyed flies (family Diopsidae) occur mostly in the Old World, with the most spectacularly broad-headed species being found in the Old World tropics. Only two species, including the *Sphyracephala brevicornis* shown here, range into the New World, and both are restricted to North America. No Diopsidae occur in the New World tropics, but other families such as the Richardiidae and Ulidiidae have evolved similarly stalk-eyed forms in South and Central America.

# Syringogastrid Fly

The Syringogastridae is a small neotropical fly family with only one genus (*Syringogaster*) of 20 species. This fly had no name when it was photographed in Bolivia in 2007 but it has now been named *Syringogaster atricalyx*. Adults are often seen on leaf surfaces along with the stinging ants they so closely resemble (they are probably mimics of *Pseudomyrmex* ants), but larvae remain unknown.

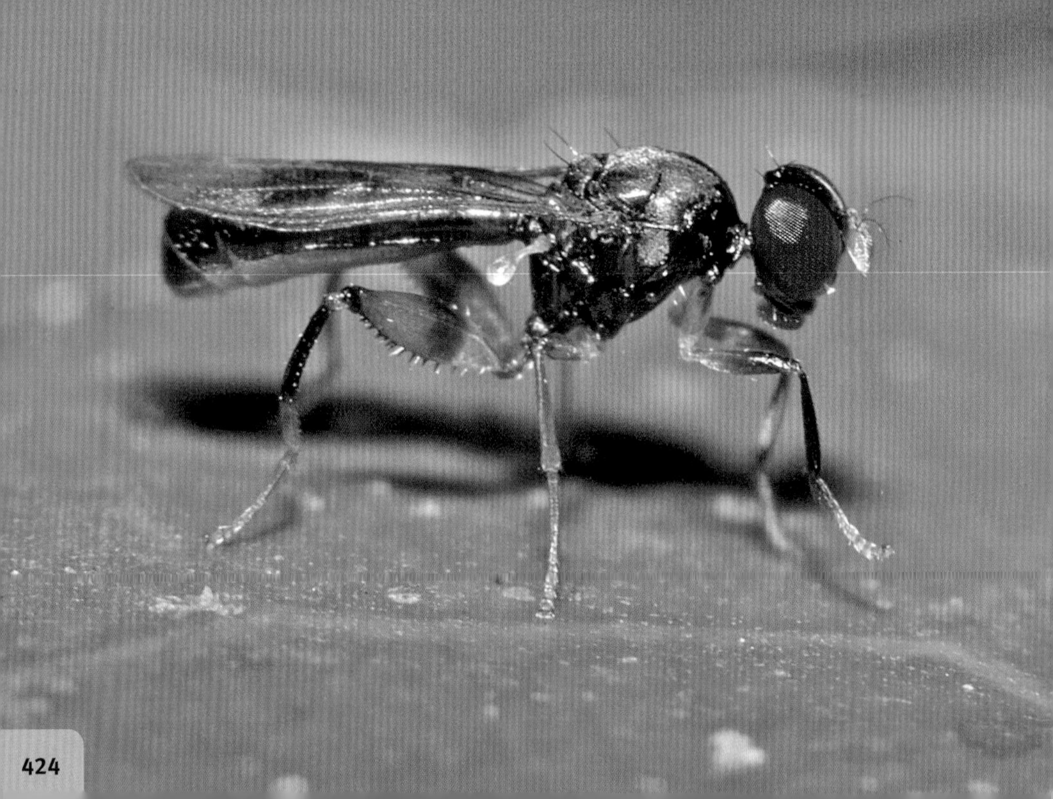

# Acalyptrate Fly



Some of the smaller families of flies are made up of inconspicuous species with odd distributions and even odder habits. Perhaps the most peculiar of these are the "upside-down flies" (family Neurochaetidae), such as this *Nothoasteia clausa* (left) from (of course) down under. Upside-down flies are best known from Australia, but they also occur in Zimbabwe, Madagascar, Malaysia and New Guinea. This one is taking its normal head-down position on its normal host, a Western Australian tall grass tree (Xanthorrhoeaceae, known in Australia as black boys). The other two slender flies shown here are also relatively poorly known acalyptrate families, a *Teratomyza undulata* (family Teratomyzidae) on an Australian tree trunk (center) and an *Aulacigaster ecuadoriensis* (family Aulacigastridae) on an Ecuadorian *Heliconia* leaf (right). The latter fly is a species that reacts to disturbance by raising its abdomen and running rapidly in a good imitation of a similarly elongate rove beetle.

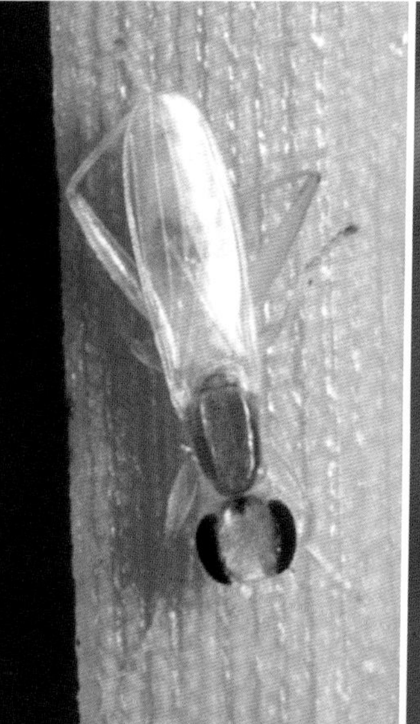

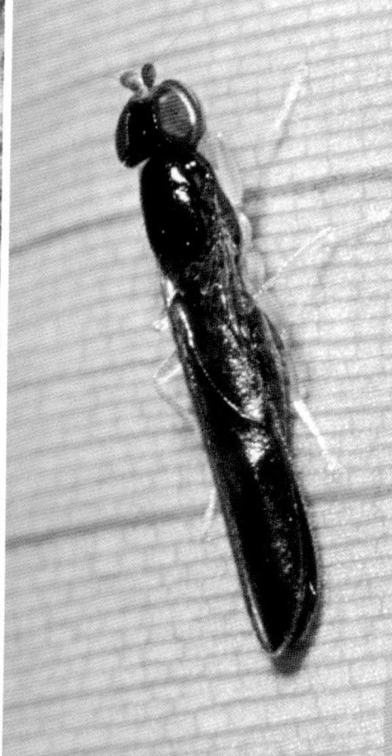

# Seaweed Fly

Very few insect families are as entirely habitat-restricted as the Coelopidae, or seaweed flies, found in piles of marine algae along rocky shorelines the world over. These flattened, hairy flies are virtually unwettable, and they are able to slip in and out of the sticky decomposing kelp with amazing speed.

# Helosciomyzid Fly

The family Helosciomyzidae is almost entirely restricted to Australia and New Zealand, but the presence of two species in southern South America suggests that this is a very old family that predates the breakup of the ancient southern continent of Gondwana. This is a *Napaeosciomyza* from New Zealand. Despite the suggestive name and a superficial similarity to the more common and widespread snail-killing flies (family Sciomyzidae), helosciomyzids apparently develop in decomposing material and are probably not closely related to Sciomyzidae.

# Titicaca Dung Fly

The family Scathophagidae is a generally north temperate group, with many common species in Europe and North America. This pilose pair of *Scathophaga tropicalis*, photographed along the Bolivian shores of Lake Titicaca, represents the only scathophagid species in southern South America. The smaller but somewhat similar Pilose Yellow Dung Fly, *Scathophaga stercoraria*, is a common meadow-muffin dweller throughout Europe and North America.

# Snail-killing Blow Fly

Most flies in the family Calliphoridae are either metallic-looking blowflies that lay their eggs on dead bodies and other decomposing material or dull-colored cluster flies that develop on earthworms. This brilliantly green *Amenia imperialis* (inset) and this metallic black-and-white *Amenia nigromaculata*, however, are Australian Calliphoridae in the unusual subfamily Ameniinae. Members of this subfamily (at least, the few with known life cycles) deposit single late-stage larvae rather than eggs; the larvae then proceed to penetrate and parasitize snails.

# Satellite Fly

Female satellite flies (subfamily Miltogramminae, family Sarcophagidae) are almost invariably seen following or circling solitary hunting wasps or lurking about their nests, waiting for an opportunity to place an egg or larva where it can develop on the paralyzed prey used by the hunting wasps (families Crabronidae and Sphecidae) to stock their nests. Males, of course, have different habits; this male *Euaraba tergata*, a widespread North American species, was photographed on a prominent perch on a New Mexico rock, from which it flew off when disturbed but always returned to keep an eye out for incoming females.

# Pitcher Plant Flesh Fly

The distinctively gray and black striped flesh fly (family Sarcophagidae) peering down into the contents of a carnivorous pitcher plant would appear to be taking a terrible risk, since most insects entering pitcher plants are on a one-way trip to the soup of half-dissolved insects in the bottom of the pitcher. Some species of flies, however, such as this *Fletcherimyia*, are specialized pitcher plant inhabitants; this fly developed as a solitary carnivorous larva within such a plant.

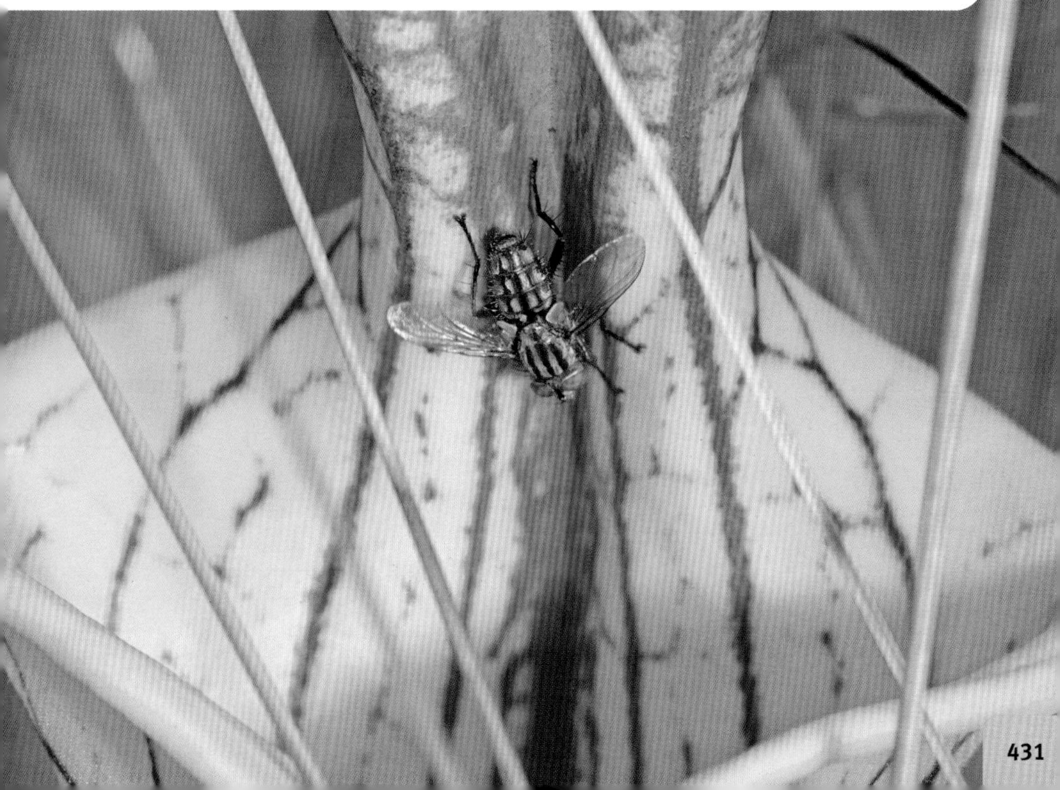

# Parasitic Fly

This *Calodexia* (subfamily Dexiinae, family Tachinidae) is perched over a swarm front of the army ant *Eciton burchellii* in Bolivia, waiting for the ants to flush out an appropriate insect host. Many species of *Calodexia*, as well as some other Tachinidae, are specialized associates of *Eciton* and are almost invariably seen in numbers around the raiding ants. All Tachinidae are parasitoids of other arthropods, and most species of *Calodexia* with known hosts attack cockroaches or crickets.

# Parasitic Fly

*Euchaetogyne roederi*, the only species in the genus *Euchaetogyne* (subfamily Dexiinae, family Tachinidae), occurs in Mexico and the southwestern United States. This one was attracted to some honey and water sprayed on oak foliage in an Arizona canyon. Many flies, especially parasitic flies in the family Tachinidae, rely on honeydew (sweet waste products egested by aphids and many other bugs) as a source of energy, and are readily attracted to sugary foliage.

# Parasitic Fly

This *Uramya halisidotae* perching on a prominent streamside rock in an Arizona canyon is a male, despite the peculiar ovipositor-like tubular tip to his abdomen. This parasitoid of caterpillars such as tent caterpillars and tiger moths has active first-stage larvae that seek out and penetrate hosts, as is typical for the subfamily Dexiinae (family Tachinidae).

# Parasitic Fly

Most of the 75 or so species of *Belvosia* (tribe Goniini, subfamily Exoristinae, family Tachinidae), such as this one from Bolivia, are distinctively robust, almost bumblebee-like flies. As is typical for the tribe Goniini, they lay small (microtype) eggs on leaves where they are likely to be accidentally eaten by moth caterpillars feeding on the foliage. Once ingested by an appropriate species, the nascent parasitic fly waits until the caterpillar has matured before embarking on a burst of development, consuming its host (by then a pupa) from the inside. Most *Belvosia* species live in South and Central America, but some range as far north as Canada.

# Parasitic Fly

The brilliant green metallic dusting on species of *Chrysexorista*, such as these flies from Ecuador (inset) and the southern United States, makes this group one of the most easily recognized genera in the enormous family Tachinidae. Like all tachinids, they are parasitoids. Like other members of one subgroup in the Exoristinae—tribe Goniini—they have a remarkable way of getting at their caterpillar hosts. Huge numbers of tiny eggs, called microtype eggs, are scattered over their hosts' food. If the correct host ingests the fly eggs, they hatch and the fly larvae consume the host from the inside.

# Parasitic Fly



This Peruvian *Patelloa* (tribe Goniini, subfamily Exoristinae, family Tachinidae) probably developed as an internal parasitoid of a large caterpillar. Members of this genus, which occurs in North America as well as Central and South America, develop as parasitoids inside the larvae of several families of moths.

# Parasitic Fly

The family Tachinidae vies with the Tipulidae for the honor of being the most speciose family of flies on the planet, and many of the 8,000 or so named species are difficult for most people to identify. This ridiculously long-legged *Cholomyia inaequipes* (tribe Myiophasiini, subfamily Tachininae) is an exception, since it is the only North American *Cholomyia* and is instantly recognizable. All tachinids are parasitic, and this one is a specialized parasitoid of weevils.

# Parasitic Fly

Orchids, milkweed and a variety of other plants literally stick it to flower-visiting insects with tacky packages of pollen grains called pollinia. This parasitic Peruvian fly (*Carcelia montana*, tribe Eryciini, subfamily Tachininae, family Tachinidae) is carrying an orchid pollinium front and center, projecting from its thorax over its head. Like most related tachinids, *Carcelia* is a parasitoid of caterpillars. This fly probably developed as a parasitoid of a large caterpillar such as a tiger or tussock moth larva.

# Parasitic Fly

This spectacular tachinid from Central America and Mexico is *Hystricia amoena*, a member of a mostly South American genus that also includes eastern North America's most spectacular tachinid, *H. abrupta*, which ranges all the way to Canada. *Hystricia* is in the subfamily Tachininae along with most of the other "big fuzzy" tachinids, but it is in the tribe Polideini (most of the really big and bristly New World tachinids are in the tribe Tachinini).

# Parasitic Fly



The big, broad parasitic flies of the genus *Macromyia* (tribe Nemoraeini, subfamily Tachininae, family Tachinidae) are mostly neotropical, but one species, *Macromya crocata*, ranges from Brazil all the way to the southwestern United States; this one was photographed in New Mexico, where it developed as a parasitoid of a large caterpillar such as a tiger or tussock moth larva.

# Parasitic Fly

*Ginglymia johnsoni* (tribe Leskiini, subfamily Tachininae, family Tachinidae) is a parasitoid like all tachinids. The closely related *G. acrirostris* is a specialized parasitoid of aquatic snout moths, and this species probably develops inside the larvae of small moths as well.

# Parasitic Fly

As its name, *Fasslomyia fantastica*, suggests, this is a fantastic little tachinid fly (tribe Ernestiini, subfamily Tachininae) with elaborate wing and body markings. This one was photographed in Peru, where it probably developed as a parasitoid inside the larva of a silkworm moth (family Bombycidae). This is the only *Fasslomyia* species, and it is known only from the Andes in Peru, Bolivia and Ecuador.

# Hedgehog Fly

The entirely parasitic family Tachinidae is one of the largest families of flies (possibly *the* largest family); its total number of named species is about 8,000 and steadily rising. Many more species in the tropics remain to be described, and new discoveries are not unusual even among larger species in North America. This southwestern American species, *Pararchytas apache*, was named by American entomologist Norman Woodley just a few years ago, in 1998. Like a wide variety of other parasitic flies, including the other "big fuzzy" Tachinidae on the following pages, *Pararchytas* is in the so-called typical tachinid subfamily Tachininae and the typical tribe Tachinini.

# Hedgehog Fly

This *Epalpus confluens* was one of many Tachinidae visiting flowers in the high Andes of Peru, along with the usual rainbow of other parasitic flies in the tribe Tachinini, alias "hedgehog flies" or big fuzzies. Larvae develop as internal parasitoids of moth caterpillars, killing their hosts in the process.

# Hedgehog Fly

Species of the genus *Epalpus* are usually the most common and diverse of the "big fuzzy" parasitic flies throughout the New World, especially at higher elevations in Central and South America, where they can be as abundant and bright as ornaments on a Christmas tree. These beautiful bristly flies are parasitoids that develop inside caterpillars.

# Hedgehog Fly



This bright *Lindigepalpus* was among many colorful “hedgehog flies”—big, bristly Tachinidae—found on flowers and honeydew-spattered foliage in a high Andean forest in Peru. The beauty of these adult flies belies the somewhat gruesome endoparasitic lifestyle of their caterpillar-killing larvae.

# Hedgehog Fly

The aptly named *Chromoepalpus* species, like this one in the high Andes of Peru, are among the most conspicuously colorful “hedgehog flies” in South America. The parasitic hedgehog flies, found mostly in one tribe of the family Tachinidae, often abound on flowers high in the mountains of Central and South America, at least during periods of suitably sunny weather.

# Hedgehog Fly

*Adejeania vexatrix* is a large, stiff-bristled tachinid fly (tribe Tachinini, subfamily Tachininae, family Tachinidae) with a conspicuous beak formed by elongate palpi combined with a long proboscis. This brightly colored fly ranges from Mexico to western Canada, and it has my vote as the most exotic-looking parasitic fly in North America. Similar and related “hedgehog flies” are conspicuous and diverse throughout Central and South America, especially around hilltops, where the males often aggregate to await incoming females. *A. vexatrix*, the only North American member of an otherwise southern genus, is often locally abundant on flowers. Larvae develop inside caterpillars.

# Hedgehog Fly

Neotropical members of the genus *Adejeania*, such as this species from the high Andes of Peru, have their palpi and proboscis slung like a huge weapon beneath the head, but of course these adult parasitic flies are completely harmless, even though their larvae are deadly to host caterpillars.

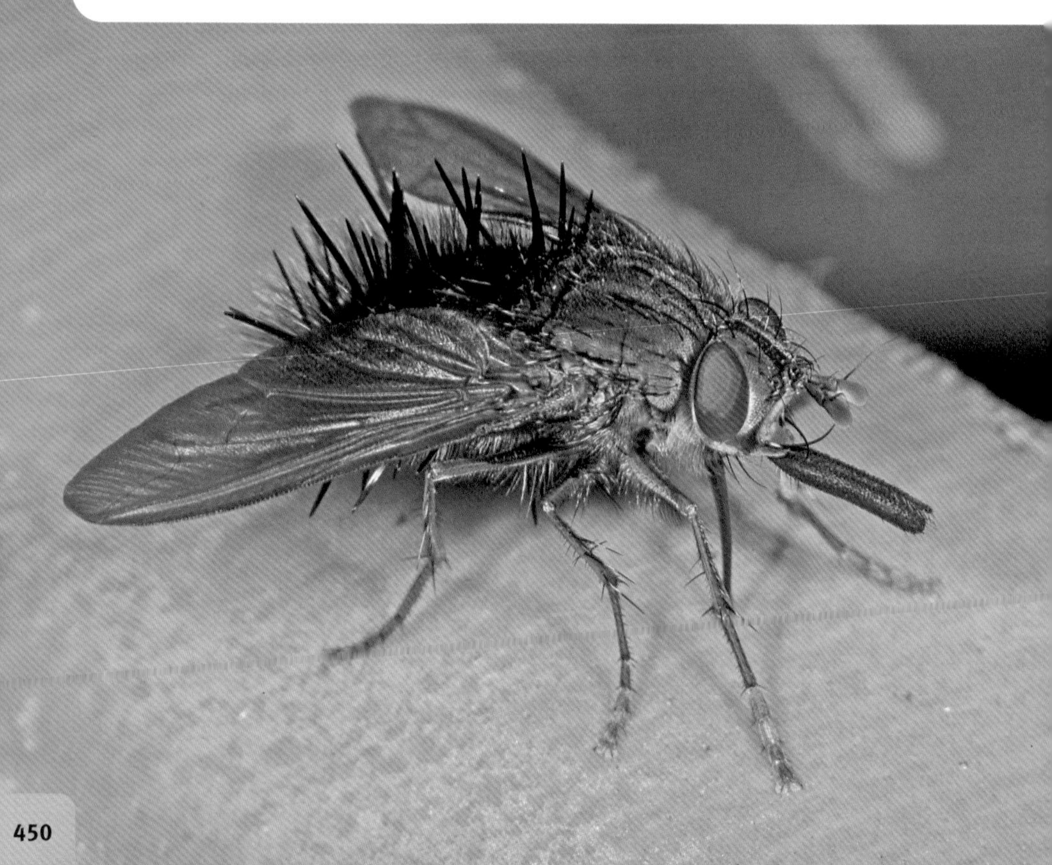

# Hedgehog Fly

This massive, black, bristly *Eudejeania pallipes* and another *Eudejeania* species dwarf a housefly-sized fly visiting the same oozing tree trunk. These impressive parasitic flies (family Tachinidae) develop inside caterpillars (large ones!).

# Hedgehog Fly

*Protodejeania* is a genus of "hedgehog flies" (tribe Tachinini, family Tachinidae) that is restricted mostly to Mexico and Central America, but this is one of the species that occurs in the American southwest.

# Bot Fly



Adult rabbit and rodent bot flies (*Cuterebra* spp., family Oestridae) are large, bee-like flies that lack functional mouthparts. Eggs are laid near rabbit or other rodent nests or runs, where the warmth of a passing host triggers hatching into a maggot that invades the animal through its mouth or nose. The bot maggot then migrates through the host's tissues to develop under the skin, breathing through a puncture that is later enlarged to allow the maggot to pop out prior to pupariating and transforming into an adult. This is a *Cuterebra austeni* from New Mexico.

# Human Bot Fly

This Human Bot Fly (*Dermatobia hominis*) started out life as an egg stuck to a mosquito's leg (or that of another kind of human-associated fly) at a research station in Ecuador. When the mosquito settled down to bite a student out doing research in the forest, the heat of the student's body made the botfly egg hatch into a little maggot, which promptly burrowed underneath the skin of her shoulder. She later watched a large boil-like swelling develop as the larva grew to the size of a grape under her skin, and was relieved when the larva matured and popped out, ready to pupate. This photo was taken not long after the adult fly had emerged from the pupa and popped the lid off its pupal shelter (puparium) by blowing out the front of its head like a balloon. The front of the head is still inflated and the wings have not yet become fully spread.

# Cuckoo Wasp

The prominently punctate and magnificently metallic cuckoo wasps (family Chrysididae) are usually killers and thieves in the nests of other wasps or bees. This one, *Trichrysis tridens*, is a kleptoparasite (food thief) in the mud nests of organ-pipe mud dauber wasps from Argentina to Canada. Cuckoo wasps have no stings, but they do have a defensive ability to roll up like an armadillo.

# Parasitic Wasp

Most wasps are parasitoids that develop in or on doomed insect hosts, and many of them belong to the huge family Ichneumonidae, which has an estimated 60,000 world species. This *Digonocryptus tarsatus* is vibrating its antennae over the surface of a tree trunk in Cuba, presumably seeking a host that it will then parasitize using its long ovipositor.

# Ensign Wasp



Most families of parasitic wasps are minute insects, difficult to identify to family even under high magnification. A few parasitic wasp families, however, are so distinctive in shape they can be easily recognized by any naturalist. The abdomen of ensign wasps (family Evaniidae), such as this one from Costa Rica, is divided into an upward-pointing petiole or stem like a flagpole, and a flat, quadrate end part like a ship's flag, or ensign. The hind legs of chalcidid wasps (family Chalcididae), such as this one from Florida (inset), are conspicuously swollen. Ensign wasps are parasitoids of cockroach egg cases; chalcidids parasitize a variety of hosts.

# Parasitic Wasp and Tent Caterpillar

This Forest Tent Caterpillar, *Malacosoma disstria*, will never turn into a moth. It will instead be consumed from the inside, either by the larvae of the tiny parasitic chalcidoid wasps laying eggs in its back or by the larva of the parasitic fly (family Tachinidae) that earlier left its white, oval egg right behind the caterpillar's head.

# Trigonalid Wasp

This wasp (*Taeniogonalos gundlachii*, family Trigonalidae) is laying eggs underneath a leaf in an Arizona canyon. Her eggs will not hatch unless they are eaten along with the foliage by an herbivorous caterpillar, and even then her newly hatched larvae are doomed unless the caterpillar is then parasitized by a wasp or fly. If the caterpillar is parasitized by a tachinid fly or an ichneumonid wasp, the larval *Taeniogonalos* will then parasitize the parasitic larva of the fly or wasp. Members of this genus occur worldwide; this species is known from Cuba as well as from Central and North America.

# Honey Bee

The Western Honey Bee (*Apis mellifera*, family Apidae) is originally an Old World species now found throughout the world, not only in domestic colonies but also in feral ones. Honey bees sometimes disperse in swarms that include the queen and thousands of workers; the sloth-like silhouette seen here beside my son's head (inset) is such a swarm (swarming bees are docile and rarely sting). The queen is protected in the middle of the swarm as the workers seek a new home for the colony.

# Bumble Bee

This Amazonian bumble bee, *Bombus transversalis*, is a species known to form unusual walking columns from their nest into the forest, but this individual was flying from flower to flower along the edge of the Bolivian rainforest. Bumble bees (part of the family Apidae) are generally insects of cooler latitudes and altitudes; this is one of only a few tropical species.

# Bumble Bee

Bumble bees such as this spectacular Chilean species, *Bombus dahlbomi*, are social insects that form small colonies in old mouse nests and similar cavities. This species has recently declined in numbers, reminiscent of some European and North American bumble bees that have become scarce in their native ranges. Other bumble bee species have been moved around the world to assist with pollination. All bees develop on a diet of pollen, and adult bees are conspicuously important pollinators of many plants.

# Bumble Bee

This pair of bumble bees (*Bombus bimaculatus*) has just completed a late fall mating flight that has left the female with a supply of sperm she won't be able to use until the following spring. Once detached from her mate, the fat female will leave the little guy to die while she seeks a sheltered place to wait out the winter before starting a new colony as a nest-founding queen. Almost all bumble bees on the wing in early spring are nest-founding queens.

# Fork-tailed Flower Bee

The Fork-tailed Flower Bee, *Anthophora furcata*, is a digger bee (subfamily Anthophorinae, family Apidae) widespread in Europe and North America. This one is nectaring at flowers of the invasive Himalayan Balsam, *Impatiens glandulifera*, in eastern Canada. Most digger bees dig solitary burrows in the ground, but the Fork-tailed Flower Bee nests in wood.

# Long-horned Bee



This male long-horned bee (*Mellisodes* sp.) has strikingly long antennae, while the female (inset, sharing a flower with a long-horned wood borer) has more "normal" antennae. *Mellisodes* is a digger bee, one of several genera in the subfamily Anthophorinae (family Apidae) that dig solitary burrows that they stock with pollen.

# Stingless Bee

Stingless bees are often attracted to perspiration, and this Costa Rican *Paratrigona opaca* is lapping sweat from the photographer's arm. These tropical bees don't sting, but they do bite, and they can descend on you in such numbers as to become a significant nuisance. Some species add irritating mandibular secretions to their bites.

# Stingless Bee



Although most of us think of honey bees and bumble bees when we think of social bees, most species of social bees belong to a closely related group called the stingless bees (subfamily Meliponinae, family Apidae). Stingless bees are diverse throughout the tropics, and a few species, such as *Melipona beecheii*, are used as a source of honey. This is a queen *M. beecheii* in a small domestic colony in Cuba.

# Stingless Bee

Stingless bees are important pollinators, and you can see the pollen on the hind leg of this *Trigona fulviventris* touching down on a Costa Rican flower. Her load of pollen and nectar will be returned to a nest with a raised, tube-like entrance such as the *Tetragonisca angustula* nest shown here (inset), in a hollow tree in a Costa Rican city park.

# Orchid Bee

Orchid bees (subfamily Euglossinae, family Apidae) such as this Costa Rican *Euglossa* have an impressively long tongue, which is normally extended only to feed in long flowers. The name orchid bee has nothing to do with the long tongue and everything to do with the way the males depend on orchids as a source of perfumes that are presumably important in their mating behaviors.

# Leafcutter Bee

Leafcutter bees (family Megachilidae) gather pollen like most bees, but instead of using a pollen basket on the hind leg like honeybees, bumblebees and related bees, they use rows of combs underneath the abdomen to carry pollen. The loaded pollen carrier, or scopa, has turned the underside of the abdomen of this black *Megachile* into a mass of yellow. All bees eat pollen, but some lack pollen-carrying devices and steal it from other bees.

# Sweat Bee



All bees eat pollen, and those that gather their own pollen rather than stealing it from other bees are appropriately equipped for transporting their haul back to the nest, where it will serve to feed the larvae. Like most bees, this *Lasioglossum leucozonum* (family Halictidae) has pollen-holding hairs on her hind legs, here seen loaded with chicory pollen on an Ontario roadside. Some halictid bees are attracted to perspiration, so the family is sometimes referred to as "sweat bees."

# Eastern Cicada Killer

Female cicada killer wasps (family Crabronidae) are equipped with impressively large stingers that are used to paralyze cicadas. However, like most solitary wasps, they are not at all aggressive and are unlikely to sting vertebrates such as us. The paralyzed cicadas are used to stock the wasp's underground nests, one cicada for a nest with a male egg and two or three for a nest with an egg due to develop into a female.

# Eastern Cicada Killer



This male cicada killer is less than half the size of an average female; he looks alert as he vigilantly fends off rival males at his territory, a patch of ground with underground nests likely to yield newly emerging virgin females. There are many different cicada killers; this species, the Eastern Cicada Killer, *Sphecius speciosus*, ranges from Central America through to eastern Canada.

# Thread-waisted Wasp

This female thread-waisted wasp (*Ammophila azteca*, family Sphecidae) is gripping a paralyzed caterpillar with her mandibles as she hauls it back to her nest, which probably already contains several other prey. She likely maintains a number of nests, progressively provisioning them with new caterpillars as her progeny develop, and closing up the nest entrance between visits. *Ammophila azteca* does occur in Mexico as the species name suggests, but it also ranges north to Yukon and across Canada; this one is from Ontario.

# Thread-waisted Wasp



The female of these eastern North American thread-waisted wasps (*Podalonia robusta*, family Sphecidae) hunts for cutworms (moth caterpillars), which she paralyzes with a sting. Each paralyzed caterpillar is placed in a cell at the end of a short burrow, dug after the prey is captured, and serves as food for the entire development of the wasp larva that hatches from an egg placed in the same cell. The relatively small male of this pair is gripping his mate with his mandibles; he had been doing so for some time as they flew from plant to plant, perhaps guarding her from other males. *Podalonia* species occur almost everywhere except South America.

# Thread-waisted Wasp

These thread-waisted wasps (family Sphecidae) make an unusual couple, not only because the female is gripping a katydid-like grasshopper, but also because the male is substantially larger than the female. The unusual size disparity in this South American species, *Sphex latreillei*, is probably the result of a mating strategy in which males wait for females to arrive at a nesting area (a sandy open patch of ground) with a paralyzed katydid. Arriving females are quickly mobbed by competing males, and the biggest male is likely to end up fathering the progeny placed on the paralyzed prey once the female runs the gauntlet of males and drags her katydid down her burrow.

# Steely Blue Cricket Hunter



This steely blue cricket hunter (*Chlorion* sp.) is a sphecid wasp (family Sphecidae) that, as the name suggests, hunts and paralyzes crickets with which to stock its underground nests. Females sometimes use the large burrrows of cicada killers (*Sphecius* spp.) as a sort of grand entrance to their own nest, making their burrows in the sides of the larger wasp's burrow and stocking each nest cell with a number of crickets.

# Paper Wasp

The elegant carton nests of the neotropical paper wasp *Angiopolybia pallens* (subfamily Polistinae, family Vespidae) can be found in tropical forests from Costa Rica to Bolivia. This nest, in a Bolivian rainforest, shows the typical tube-like extension with a circular entrance, guarded by a few wasps that seemed to be routinely engaged in chasing small flies (family Phoridae) away from the entrance. The wasps responded to a gentle poke at the nest by distributing themseves evenly over its surface (right). Other neotropical paper wasps can be much more aggressive—even a gentle nest poke is not generally a good idea!

# Paper Wasp

Paper wasps are predators and scavengers that feed on a wide variety of high-protein material, which is usually masticated into a pulp before it is returned to the nest. Some are strongy attracted to vertebrate carrion, but most hunt other insects and chew them up like the mass being masticated by this Bolivian paper wasp.

# Paper Wasp

Like many tropical paper wasps, but unlike the familiar North American Polistinae, the small neotropical social wasps in the genus *Protopolybia* start new paper nests as coordinated groups of queens (reproductive females) and workers (non-reproductive females). The genus *Protopolybia* (subfamily Polistinae, family Vespidae) is restricted to the neotropics; these *P. amarella* workers were photographed in Bolivia.

# Western Paper Wasp

*Mischocyttarus* (subfamily Polistinae, family Vespidae) is a mostly neotropical genus with only four species, including this yellow-legged Western Paper Wasp, *Mischocyttarus navajo*, in the United States. As is also true for the more familiar *Polistes* paper wasps, the queen lays her eggs in cells (eggs are visible in the upper cells of this photograph) and the developing larvae (visible in the middle cells) are fed insect prey. *Mischocyttarus* species look much like *Polistes* but have a long, narrow "wasp waist."

# Paper Wasp

Paper wasps in the genus *Polistes* are the most familiar paper wasps, with over 200 species scattered around the world. This large *Polistes carnifex* queen is protecting her nest in a Costa Rican rainforest. Her brood cells are capped now, and about to yield a new generation of workers that developed from larvae in the open cells, fed regularly on a diet of masticated prey. All *Polistes* gather arthropod prey, often caterpillars, and all make open paper nests.

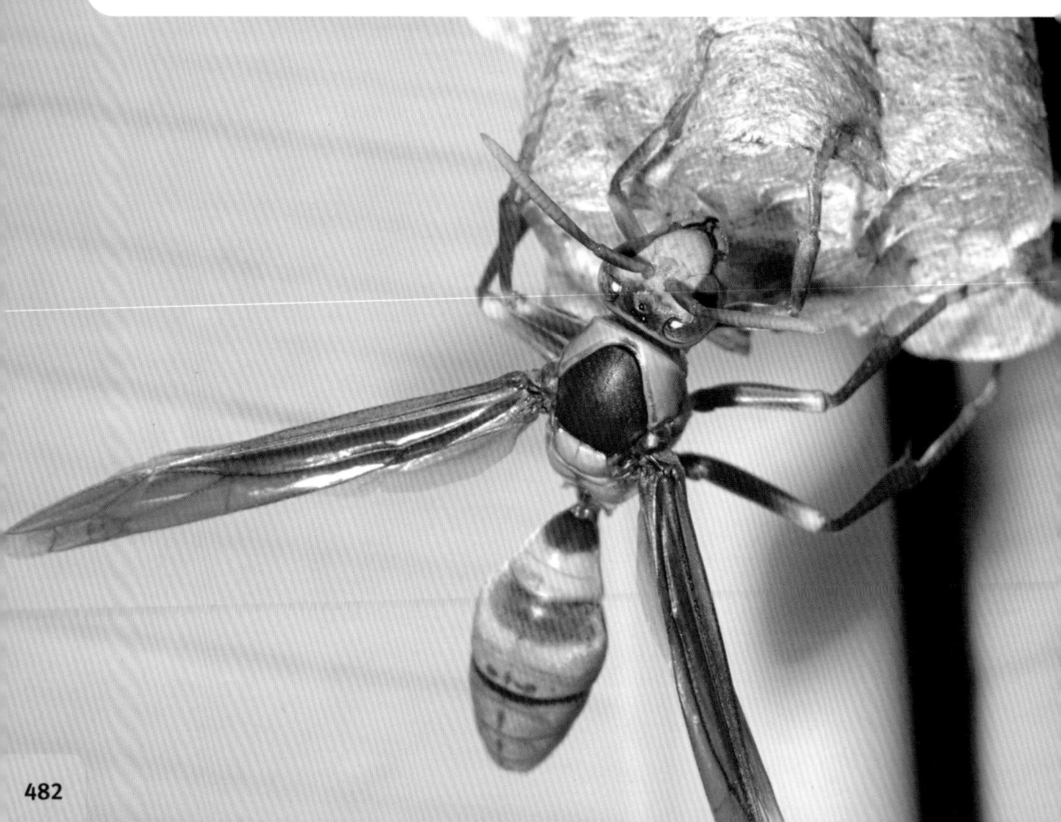

# European Paper Wasp



Paper wasps in the genus *Polistes* (subfamily Polistinae, family Vespidae) live in relatively small colonies. As a rule they make open nests that usually hang from a narrow stem, although this *Polistes dominula* nest sticking out of the end of a metal pipe seems to break that rule. *P. dominula* is an invasive wasp recently introduced to North America, where it is thriving despite competition from many native species.

# Aerial Yellowjacket

Yellowjacket wasps (subfamily Vespinae, family Vespidae) are social wasps that readily use their stings to defend their colonies, in doing so often coming into conflict with people. These wasps peering suspiciously from the entrance at the bottom of a large paper nest in a Canadian city backyard belong to the common species *Dolichovespula arenaria*, or Aerial Yellowjacket.

# Aerial Yellowjacket



This Aerial Yellowjacket, *Dolichovespula arenaria*, has just swept in to grab a small moth. Now, only seconds after the attack, the only evidence of the moth is a flurry of scales besmirching the attacking wasp and a barely recognizable mangled body about to be masticated by the wasp's mandibles. She will take the resulting mash back to her paper nest to feed colony larvae. This is an abundant North American species and the architect of the most common enclosed paper nests in eastern North America.

# Western Yellowjacket

Despite its misleading species name, the Western Yellowjacket, *Vespula pensylvanica*, is indeed western, and one of the most common and aggressive wasps in western North America. This one attacked a large robber fly that had itself just grabbed a beetle (a rose chafer); the robber fly beat a hasty retreat, leaving the wasp to sting the beetle before ripping it to shreds for transport back to her nest. Western Yellowjackets are now invasive pests in Hawaii.

# Spider Wasp

Spider wasps (family Pompilidae) are solitary wasps that hunt and paralyze spiders, usually dragging them into underground nests to serve as hosts for the wasp's larvae. Most spider wasps are black, but this *Tachypompilus ferrugineus*, on a goldenrod flower in South Carolina, is a conspicuous exception. Large spider wasps like this one, which hunts wolf spiders, or the really large *Pepsis* wasps, which hunt tarantulas, have frighteningly large stings. It is a good thing that these wasps, like most solitary wasps, are not aggressive, and rarely sting vertebrates.

# Spider Wasp

Most spider wasp females (family Pompilidae) use their stingers to subdue arachnid prey, usually dragging the stung and paralyzed spider into a nest (often a burrow). There it will serve as prey for a wasp larva that hatches from a single egg laid on the spider's abdomen before it is entombed in the wasp's nest. This spider wasp from Western Australia is *Calopompilus raptor*.

# Tarantula Hawk

This tarantula hawk (*Pepsis* sp.) is a spider wasp (family Pompilidae) that has what it takes to subdue tarantulas—*Pepsis* stingers can be as long as 0.3 inch (7 mm) and they pack a potent venom. The bright orange wings warn potential predators to stay away, and they are imitated by a variety of harmless insects (especially flies) that presumably gain some protection by pretending to be these powerful wasps. Female tarantulas, often wrenched from their burrows, are paralyzed and dragged back to the female wasp's burrow, where they serve as food for her larvae. This wasp was photographed in New Mexico, where a tarantula hawk is the official state insect.

# Spider Wasp

This unusual-looking Bolivian spider wasp (family Pompilidae) belongs to the genus *Euplaniceps*. A few spider wasps allow their spider hosts to go about their business while the spider wasp larva develops as an ectoparasitoid on the mobile host, but most hunt and paralyze their prey, immobilizing each spider prior to sealing it in a nest with a single wasp egg. Some specialize in taking over spider prey from other spider wasps.

# Chyphotid Wasp

Wasps in the small family Chyphotidae, until recently treated as part of the Bradynobaenidae, resemble velvet ants. This is a male *Chyphotes* from Arizona. Like velvet ants (family Mutillidae), only the males have wings, and the wingless females look like ants. The winged males are nocturnal (look at those ocelli, typical of nocturnal wasps) and sometimes show up at lights in arid areas. Not much is known about the biology of these obscure insects, but they are thought to parasitize sun scorpions (order Solifugae, class Arachnida).

# Velvet Ant

Velvet ants (family Mutillidae) are wasps with heavily armored, impressively armed wingless females and innocuous flying males. Most velvet ants, such as this *Hoplomutilla* (inset) zipping over the sand along the banks of an Amazon tributary, are seen on open ground, where they seek hosts such as ground-nesting wasps. Others, probably including this Costa Rican *Pseudomethoca* running across a leaf, develop in the nests of solitary bees.

# Velvet Ant

North America's most spectacular velvet ants (family Mutillidae) belong to the speciose genus *Dasymutilla* (around 150 species), which are widely known as "cow killers" because of the wicked-looking stingers packed by their huge, hairy, wingless females. This *Dasymutilla klugii*, photographed in New Mexico, is a parasitoid in the ground nests of an enormous cicada-hunting wasp, the Western Cicada Killer, *Sphecius grandis*.

# Dolichoderus Ant

These *Dolichoderus* ants scavenging on a dead moth in Bolivia possibly belong to an as-yet-undescribed species still to be added to the 170 or so described species (including several known only from fossils) of this genus worldwide. *Dolichoderus* species are general scavengers that are often found lapping up sweet fluids from extrafloral nectaries or from honeydew-egesting aphids and planthoppers. The ant family (Formicidae) is routinely divided into subfamilies, and *Dolichoderus* is the typical genus of the subfamily Dolichoderinae.

# Leaf-cutting Ant



The fungus-gardening or leaf-cutting ants (tribe Attini, subfamily Myrmicinae) are the archetypal insects of the New World tropics, where these extraordinary—and extraordinarily abundant—insects are the most important plant pests. Leafcutter ants cut out leaf fragments to carry back to their large subterranean nests, where they are used to grow fungus for food. Not all members of the leaf-cutting tribe Attini are tropical; this *Trachymyrmex septentrionalis* is carrying a leaf in a South Carolina oak forest. *T. septentrionalis* behaves much like the famous neotropical leaf-cutting ants in the genus *Atta*, but inconspicuously and on a smaller scale.

# Leaf-cutting Ant

This Costa Rican leaf-cutting ant (*Acromyrmex* sp., tribe Attini, subfamily Myrmicinae) begs to be called by the alternative common name applied to this tribe: parasol ants. Whether the cargo is a parasol-like flower or the more usual cut-out leaf fragment, the destination is a huge underground nest where the payload will be "composted" into a fungus garden.

# Leaf-cutting Ant

These Bolivian ants belong to the most common group of leaf-cutting ants, the genus *Atta*, which ranges from the southern United States to southern South America. Leafcutter ants are plagued by little flies (genus *Apocephalus*, family Phoridae, inset) that parasitize worker ants, injecting them with eggs that develop into larvae that consume their hosts from the inside, ultimately killing them (and often decapitating the ants in the process, pupating in the detached head capsule). The aggressive-looking ants riding on this leaf fragment are guards that fend off ant-decapitating flies.

# Megalomyrmex Ant

This *Megalomyrmex balzani* is imbibing sweet fluids from an extrafloral nectary on an *Inga* leaf in Bolivia. Plants produce extrafloral nectaries—essentially pots of sweet plant exudate—specifically to attract ants that will protect them from foliage-eating insects. *Megalomyrmex* is a strictly neotropical genus, with about 30 species, including some thought to be specialized associates or predators of small leafcutter ants.

# Big-headed Ant

The big-headed ants (*Pheidole* spp.) form an enormously diverse group, with about 900 named species worldwide, of which more than half were recently discovered and named by Edward O. Wilson, ant taxonomist and arguably the most widely known and respected biologist of our time. These two Arizona *Pheidole* illustrate the huge differences between sisters (workers from the same colony). The big-headed "major" worker in the foreground is more of a nutcracker than a soldier; it functions to carry and break up seeds and other food items. *Pheidole* species, like the more conspicuous *Pogonomyrmex* species, are often called harvester ants; both are especially important seed consumers in the American southwest.

# Harvester Ant

*Pogonomyrmex* ants are the most familiar harvester ants, with about 22 American species, including the common Red Harvester Ants of the southwest. Red Harvester Ants, *P. barbatus*, form large colonies in conspicuous open patches that are kept free of vegetation by the worker ants. If you see one of these ants hauling a seed or a dead insect back to its nest, leave it alone—"pogos" have powerful stings that pack a painful wallop. That sting is also worth keeping in mind the next time you see an ant farm for sale, since harvester ants are often sold with them.

# Acrobat Ant and Leaf-mining Fly

*Crematogaster* ants, familiar for their heart-shaped abdomens, are sometimes called acrobat ants because the worker ants often carry their abdomen above the rest of the body, as though performing a balancing act. These little ants are abundant and diverse worldwide, and are often the dominant ants in a wide variety of forests. They feed on both living and dead insects as well as sugar sources such as honeydew; this Bolivian ant is sharing a honeydew-spattered leaf with a leaf-mining fly (family Agromyzidae).

# Gliding Ant

Lots of ants live in trees, where it helps to be able to leap like a lemur or a flying squirrel. *Cephalotes* ants, like these from Costa Rica, are known as gliding ants because of their ability to glide back to their home trees when dislodged or chased into the air. They visually orient to the tree trunk and then use their flat head and body projections to make a sort of directed skydive back to base.

# Cuban Ant



Cuba is home to many endemic ants that have evolved in the isolation of that large Caribbean island, and a couple of dozen of the Cuba-only species are thought to be descended from a single immigrant ancestor. This *Temnothorax mortoni* is one of the remarkable island-bound species that today stand as evidence of a spectacular evolutionary radiation.

# Green Weaver Ant

These Australian Green Weaver Ants, *Oecophylla smaragdina*, are scurrying over a silken net spun between leaves to make a tent-like structure to house their colony. The woven nest of silk and living leaves is all the more remarkable because it was created by worker ants holding silk-producing larvae like living bobbins to glue together leaves held in place by chains of other workers. Colonies can grow to immense size and often span several trees. Like carpenter ants and other members of the ant subfamily Formicinae, these ants cannot sting, but they can bite and then exacerbate the pain of the bite with a squirt of formic acid.

# Common Black Ant

Like many other ants, *Formica* species frequently tend aphids and related honeydew-producing bugs for their sweet waste products. Aphids tended by ants are much less likely to be attacked by parasitic wasps than those without ant shepherds.

# Elongate Twig Ant

The Elongate Twig Ant (*Pseudomyrmex gracilis*) was accidentally introduced from Mexico to the southeastern United States, and can now be found throughout much of Florida and southern Texas. This one is stinging (inset) and capturing a small barklouse (Psocoptera), but twig ant's stings are also sometimes used against people unlucky enough to brush against hollow twigs housing the small nests of this species.

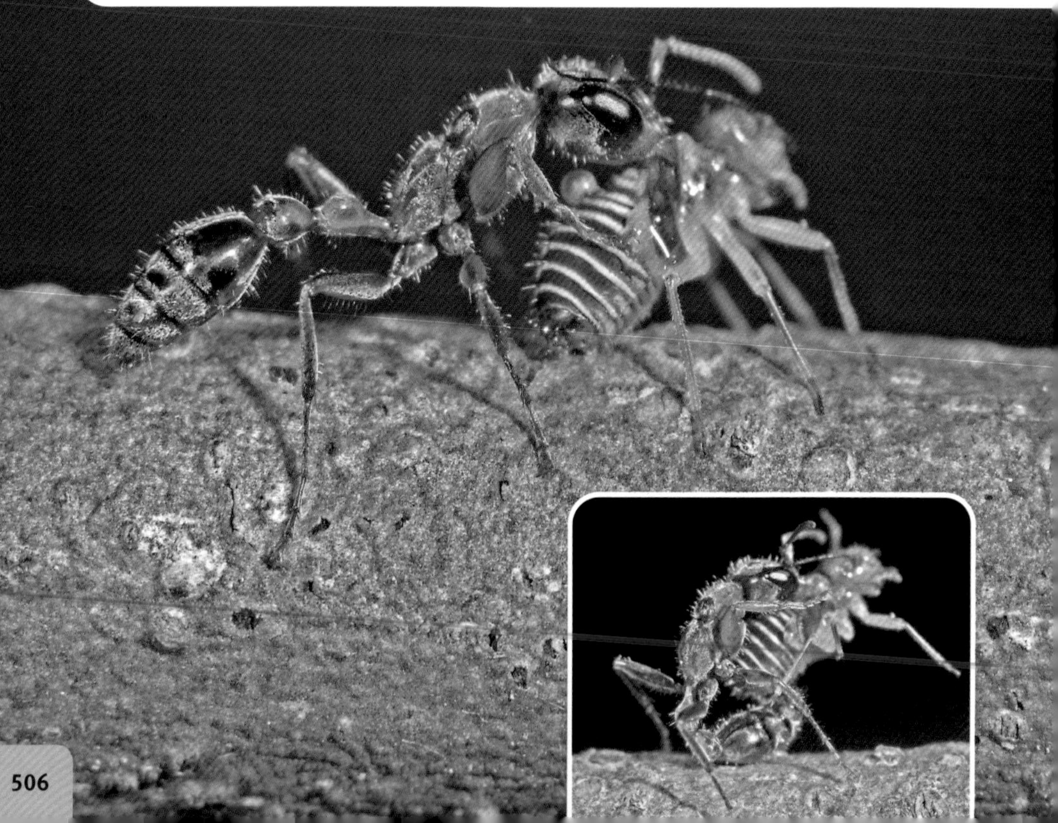

# Golden Carpenter Ant



This Golden Carpenter Ant (*Camponotus sericeiventris*) is striking a defensive pose over a dead moth in Cost Rica. The carpenter ant genus is a huge one, with many difficult to identify species, but the Golden Carpenter Ant is one of the more common and distinctive neotropical ants all the way from Mexico to Argentina.

# Carpenter Ant

Although the genus *Camponotus* is best known for a few pest species of carpenter ants, this enormous and widespread genus of about a thousand species varies widely in biology and appearance. This winged reproductive (inset), for example, is a specialized Amazonian species, *Camponotus mirabilis*, that lives inside live Guadua bamboo, modifying the stems with holes and wicks made from wood fiber to create a dry home for the colony. This wingless ant is a *Camponotus* worker of another species from the same Amazonian forest.

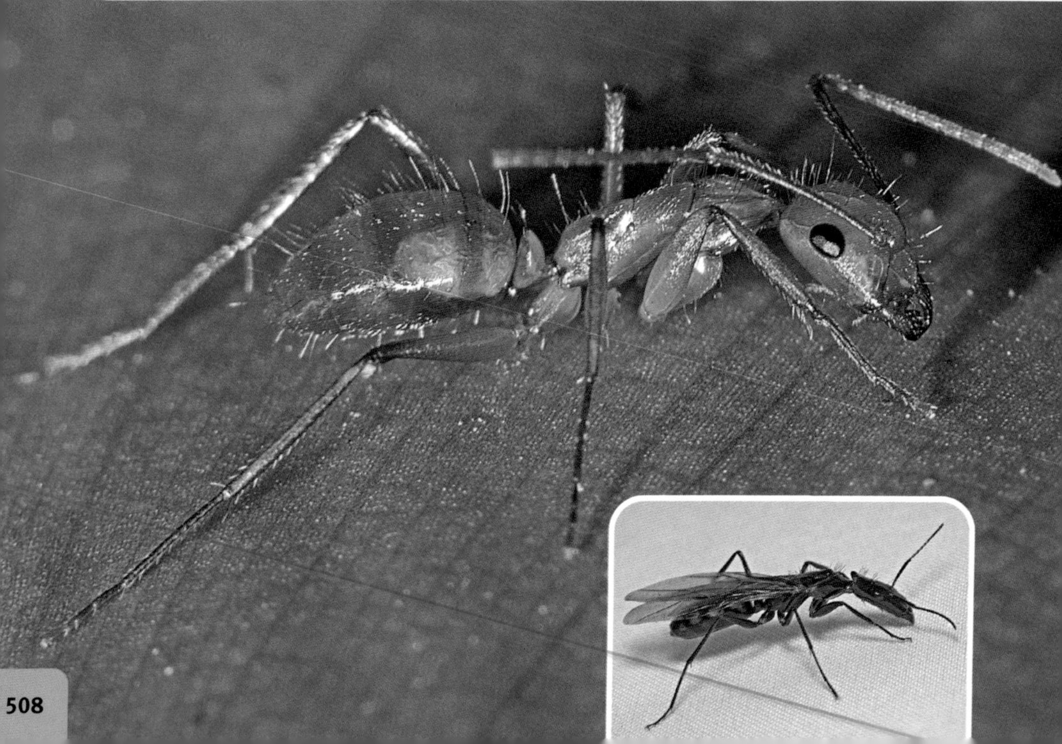

# Kelep



Keleps, *Ectatomma tuberculatum*, are common ants from Mexico south to Brazil, where single ants can usually be found defending extrafloral nectaries or hunting for other insects on the foliage. This one is waiting to ambush flies coming in to a bit of dung on a lichen-spattered tree trunk. Like other solitary hunting ants in the subfamily Ponerinae, these big ants can sting, but their sting is not as painful as that of the related *Paraponera clavata*.

# Bullet Ant

*Paraponera clavata* is an intimidatingly large and well-armed ant found from Central America to Amazonia, widely known as the bullet ant (*bala*) because of the impact of its sting (it does feel as if you have been shot!). *P. clavata* workers aggressively guard the entrances to their small underground colonies. The ant shown here, from Bolivia, is guarding a foraging site on foliage.

# Panther Ant

Neotropical forests are rich in conspicuously large ponerine ants (subfamily Ponerinae) equipped to sting and paralyze prey such as the termite carried by this Bolivian panther ant (*Neoponera*). Some similar Amazonian ponerines, such as the descriptively named Dinosaur Ant (*Dinoponera gigantea*), are huge, with lengths that can exceed an inch (3 cm).

# Trap-jaw Ant

Some ants have long mandibles that form a snap-jaw mechanism that can spring shut virtually instantaneously (in less than a millisecond!) when potential prey stimulate special long trigger hairs. This Costa Rican *Odontomachus* has its mandibles cocked and locked wide open near a bit of monkey dung on a leaf, a good place to capture an unwary fly.

# Bulldog Ant



This bulldog ant (*Myrmecia* sp.) is looking straight at the camera, and might well have jumped at the photographer seconds later. The 90 or so species of *Myrmecia* (all Australian) are solitary hunters that use their big eyes and jumping ability to hunt other insects. These large, aggressive ants are infamous for their powerful sting; sometimes they are called jumping ants or jack ants.

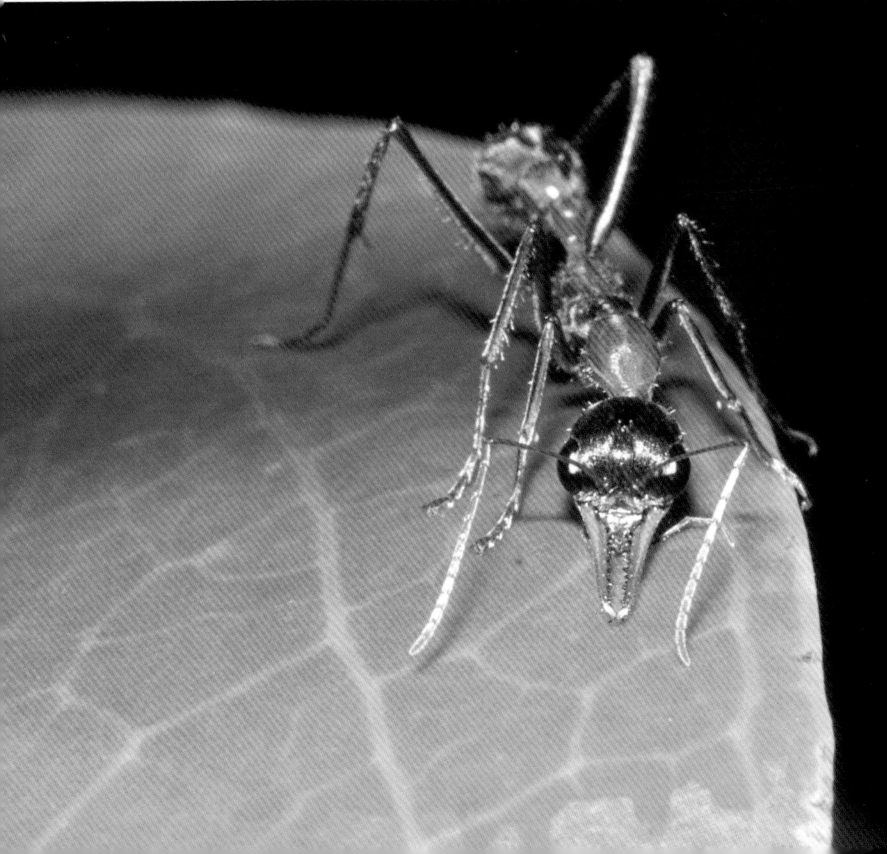

# Army Ant

The New Word army ant *Eciton hamatum* is a "column raider" that attacks the nests of other social insects from Bolivia to Mexico, swiftly marching along in neat, impressive lines of conspicuously armed soldiers and smaller-jawed workers. *Eciton* colonies are nomadic and do not have a true nest to which to return with their prey; instead they form only temporary "bivouacs" that are entirely relocated at regular intervals.

# Army Ant

The most commonly seen army ant throughout South and Central America is *Eciton burchellii*. This abundant ant raids in conspicuous swarms that inundate broad areas at the leading edge of the column, capturing almost every arthropod flushed by the swarm front. Despite the fictions perpetrated by popular literature and movies, New World army ants are not dangerous to people. However, the big jaws sported by the soldiers of some species can pierce your skin painfully; it is a good idea to tuck your pants into your boots if you plan on standing in the middle of a swarm front.

# Glossary

**bioluminescence**—production of light by living organisms; most familiar in fireflies.

**class**—Life is divided into a few kingdoms (insects are in the animal kingdom), which are divided into phyla, which are in turn divided into classes. Classes are divided into *orders* (beetles, flies, wasps and moths make up the four biggest orders), which are in turn divided into families, genera and species.

**elytra**—the hard, armor-like fore-wings of beetles (singular: elytron).

**exotic**—present in an area only because of mankind's accidental or deliberate agency.

**family**—All species are grouped into genera, which are in turn grouped into families, which are in turn grouped into orders. Most insect families are easily recognized anywhere in the world. Family names end in -idae but are often expressed informally with the ending -id; for example, ground beetles are in the family Carabidae but are often called carabids.

**genus**—a named group of related species. Every species is placed in a genus, sometimes alone but usually with closely related species.

**honeydew**—sugar-rich waste products of sap-sucking bugs such as aphids: an important source of food for many insects.

**larva**—an immature, flightless stage in the development of a winged insect or of any insect with a winged ancestor, especially an immature insect without external wing development.

**lineage**—a group of related species, all the descendents of one common ancestor.

**maggot**—the legless larva of a fly (order Diptera).

**metamorphosis**—development involving one or two special molts, usually to facilitate transformation from flightless immature stages to fully winged adults.

**molting**—periodic shedding of the rigid external skeleton to allow growth.

**myrmecophilous**—living in close association with ants.

**native**—a species that occurs naturally in an area. If it occurs only in one area and nowhere else, it is *endemic* to that area.

**neotropical**—relating to the biogeographic region that includes South America, Central America and much of Mexico.

**new species**—a species that has not yet been given a formal scientific name; also called an undescribed species.

**ovipositor**—the egg-laying tube of some female insects, located at or near the tip of the abdomen.

**parasitoid**—an organism that lives in or on another organism, killing its host. A parasite does not kill its host; a parasitoid kills a single host organism.

**predator**—an organism that kills and consumes more than one other organism.

**raptorial**—grasping, usually referring to the swollen legs used by some predaceous insects to hold prey.

**scales**—broad, flattened bristles used to impart color, insulate, expedite escape from predators, diffuse scents, and for various other functions.

**sexually dimorphic**—having a different appearance for different sexes.

**species**—the basic units of evolution, simply defined as distinct groupings of actually or potentially interbreeding individuals; the result of lineage diversification by speciation.

**sting**—the ovipositor of some female wasps that has been modified into a venom-delivery device.

# Further Reading


Castner, J.L. *Amazon Insects: A Photo Guide*. Gainesville, FL: Feline Press, 2000 (160 pages)

Eaton, E., and K. Kaufman. *Kaufman Field Guide to Insects of North America*. New York: Houghton Mifflin, 2006 (392 pages)

Eisner, T. *For Love of Insects*. Cambridge, MA: Harvard University Press, 2003 (448 pages)

Evans, A. *National Wildlife Federation Field Guide to Insects and Spiders and Related Species of North America*. New York: Sterling Publishing, 2007 (497 pages)

Grimaldi, D., and M.S. Engel. *Evolution of the Insects*. Cambridge: Cambridge University Press, 2005 (755 pages)

Hogue, C.L. *Latin American Insects and Entomology*. Berkeley: University of California Press, 1993 (594 pages)

Johnson, N.F., and C.A. Triplehorn. *Borror and DeLong's Introduction to the Study of Insects*. 7th ed. Toronto, ON: Brooks/Cole, 2004 (864 pages)

Marshall, S.A. *Beetles: The Natural History and Diversity of Coleoptera*. Toronto, ON: Firefly Books, 2018 (784 pages)

Marshall, S.A. *Flies: The Natural History and Diversity of Diptera*. Toronto, ON: Firefly Books, 2012 (616 pages)

Marshall, S.A. *Hymenoptera: The Natural History and Diversity of Wasps, Bees and Ants*. Toronto, ON: Firefly Books, 2023 (640 pages)

Marshall, S.A. *Insects: Their Natural History and Diversity*. Toronto, ON: Firefly Books, 2006 (736 pages)


# Internet Sources

Although the Web can be a tremendous resource, it can be challenging to find sites that provide reliable, useful information about insect diversity. Ironically, this problem has been exacerbated in recent years by the proliferation of well-funded and well-intentioned attempts to put up all-encompassing biodiversity websites. Most of these sites now consist primarily of links to names with no further information—sort of like giant shopping malls full of empty shelves with tantalizing labels. Web searches using taxon names (such as family, genus or species names) frequently take you to these "empty shelves." The most useful sites (those with fully stocked shelves) are put up by taxonomic experts sharing their specialized expertise, dedicated communities of enthusiasts, institutions dedicated to reliable content, or reputable journals with a focus on accessible products. An extensive list of entomological internet resources can be found at www.ent.iastate.edu/list/directory/86/vid/5.

Canadian Journal of Arthropod Identification—www.biology.ualberta.ca/bsc/ejournal/ejournal.html

BugGuide—bugguide.net/node/view/15740

Tree of Life—www.tolweb.org/Hexapoda/2528

Blattodea Culture Group—www.blattodea-culture-group.org

Earwig Research Centre—www.earwigs-online.de

Diptera.info—www.diptera.info/news.php

Odonata Information Network—www.iodonata.net

Orthoptera Species File Online—osf2.orthoptera.org/HomePage.aspx

Antbase—www.antbase.org

caterpillars.org: Caterpillars of La Selva—www.tulane.edu/~ldyer/lsacat/index.htm

Chilean Insects—www.entomologia.cl

Coleoptera.org—www.coleoptera.org

iNaturalist—https://www.inaturalist.org

# Acknowledgments

While identification of insects from temperate regions is becoming easier thanks to new field guides, monographs and websites, identification of tropical insects still remains largely the realm of specialists with access to good reference collections. I am indebted to innumerable colleagues for looking at specimens, checking images or answering questions.

My associates here at the University of Guelph insect collection were unfailingly supportive—thanks especially to Matthew Buck and Steven Paiero for their help with everything. Fellow members of the dipterist community were always willing to look at my specimens or pictures—Eric Fisher, Monty Wood, Norman Woodley, Jeff Cumming, Bohdan Bilyj, Torbjørn Ekrem, Chen Young, Scott Brooks, David Yeates, Brad Sinclair, Neal Evenhuis, Wayne Mathis, Lloyd Knutson, Jeff Skevington, Allen Norrbom, Christian Thompson, James O'Hara, Raymond Gagne, Evert Schlinger, Martin Hauser, David Yeates, John Burger, Richard Wilkerson, Steve Gaimari, Aynsley Thielman, Owen Lonsdale and Joel Kits. Lois O'Brien patiently dealt with all my questions about fulgoroids; Duane Flynne provided assistance with treehoppers and stink bugs. Andy Hamilton and Daniela Takiya identified auchenorrhych images. Dimitri Forero helped with assassin bugs, Harry Brailovsky identified some coreids, Michael Schwartz provided mirid advice, and Edwin Mockford named my neotropical psocids. I welcomed lepidopterological advice from Jean-Francois Landry, John Rawlins, Carlos Lamas, Lee Dyer, Marc Epstein, Timothy McCabe, Richard Brown, Julian Donahue and Jim Troubridge. Fabian Haas eyeballed my earwigs, Hendrik Devriese tangled with my tetrigid images, Piotr Naskrecki advised me about tettigoniids, George Beccaloni identified my cockroaches and Tim Myles told me about my termites. Christian Gonzalez helped with Chilean insects living and dead, Manuel Solis and Manuel Zumbado fed my fascination with Costa Rican insects, and José Fernández Triana and Gabriel Garces advised on Cuban insects. George Ball, Richard Freitag, Alfred Newton, Ed Riley, Paul Skelley, Zoe Simmons, Andrew Smith, Mary Liz Jameson, Steven Lingafelter, Caroline Chaboo, Patrice Bouchard, Vasily Grebennikov, Chuck Bellamy, Patrice Bouchard, Henry Stockwell, Robert Anderson, Ed Riley, Wills Flowers, Jeff Heuther, Warren Steiner, Charles Bellamy, Bruce Gill and Rob Roughley helped with matters coleopterological. Gary Umphrey, Juan Vieira, James Pitts and John Asher helped with Hymenoptera names.

I would also like to thank the participants in the 2007 field entomology course for sharing their enthusiasm for the fantastic insects of the Bolivian rainforest, many of which appear in this book.

# Index

Insect families are listed in **bold** type; they include subfamilies, tribes and genera (see page 14 for an explanation of how classification works). Page numbers in **bold** type indicate photographs in the Introduction.